THE SUPER EASY TEEN CHEF COOKBOOK

1500 Days of Effortless and Flavorful Creations for Young Culinary Enthusiasts to Master the Skills in the Kitchen | Full Colour Edition

Janet D. Saucedo

Manufactured in the United States of America
Interior and Cover Designer: Danielle Rees
Art Producer: Brooke White
Editor: Aaliyah Lyons
Production Editor: Sienna Adams
Production Manager: Sarah Johnson
Photography: Michael Smith

TABLE OF CONTENTS

TABLE OF CONTENTS

INTRODUCTION

Me and my 7-year-old sidekick, Sophia, turning our kitchen into a total adventure zone – and loving every single minute of it. When a second-grader decides she's going to be a cooking master, things are about to get seriously interesting.

Let's be honest – I never thought I'd be the type of parent who'd let an elementary school kid take over the kitchen. Sharp knives? Hot surfaces? Seemed like a recipe for disaster. But then Sophia happened. One day, she walks into the kitchen with this look of total determination, pulls up her step stool, and announces she's ready to become a real chef. Her confidence? Totally impressive. My nervousness? Through the roof.

We started with the classic beginner's challenge: cookies. Because cookies are basically the ultimate cooking gateway for kids who want to prove they're kitchen pros.

Sophia's first attempts were a mix of precision and pure chaos. Her measuring might not have been perfect, but her enthusiasm was 100% on point. She'd carefully crack eggs (mostly into the bowl), mix ingredients with this super-serious concentration face, and then look up with this proud grin that could melt any parent's heart.

As weeks went by, Sophia's skills started to level up. She went from random ingredient flinger to actual sous-chef material. Her apron became her official chef uniform, and she started giving me actual cooking advice. Who knew a 7-year-old could have such strong opinions about the right way to mix cookie dough?

We tackled increasingly ambitious projects. Peanut butter sandwiches? Old news. Homemade pasta? Bring it on. Our "world's longest noodle" attempts became legendary family stories – half art project, half cooking experiment, totally hilarious.

Our kitchen sessions were never just about food. They were about:

- Learning to follow (and sometimes creatively interpret) recipes
- Understanding that mistakes are just part of learning
- Discovering that cooking is part science, part magic, and mostly fun

The cleaning up became another challenge we'd tackle together. Sophia discovered that dish duty could be its own kind of game, turning chores into something almost – dare I say – enjoyable?

Every time she looks up and asks, "Mom, what complicated recipe can we try next?" I know we're creating something way more important than just a meal. We're building memories, skills, and a relationship that goes way beyond the kitchen.

DEDICATION

To Sophia,

You're my kitchen adventure partner, my young chef with big dreams. This book is our story—a collection of recipes, laughs, and the kind of memories that make parenting the most incredible journey. Here's to our culinary chaos and all the amazing moments yet to come.

Love,
Mom.

CHAPTER 1: LET'S GET COOKING!

STAY SAFE, STAY COOL: KITCHEN VIBES!

Get ready to dive into the ultimate guide to keeping it chill and safe while you work your culinary magic. Let's turn up the tunes and groove in the kitchen as we explore the essentials of staying safe and cool while cooking up a storm!

Safety in the kitchen isn't just about following rules – it's about creating a vibe that's all about fun, creativity, and keeping things running smoothly. So let's kick things off by talking about why safety is the ultimate ingredient for a successful cooking session.

Picture this: you're whipping up your favorite dish, totally in the zone, when suddenly... oops! A little slip-up could lead to a major bummer. But fear not, my fellow foodies! With a few simple tips and tricks, you'll be navigating the kitchen like a pro in no time.

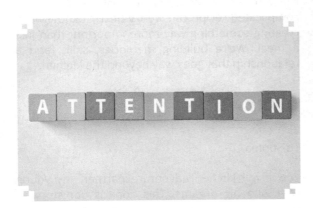

Tip #1: Keep it Clean, Keep it Fresh

Alright, let's kick things off with some hygiene 101. A clean kitchen is a happy kitchen, so roll up those sleeves and get scrubbing! Wash your hands thoroughly and give those countertops a good wipe-down too. Remember, cleanliness is key to keeping those kitchen vibes chill and oh-so-fresh.

Tip #2: Master the Art of Knife Safety

Now, let's talk about everyone's favorite kitchen tool: the mighty knife. Sharp and oh-so-powerful, but also a potential hazard if not handled with care. Start by choosing the right knife for the job – a dull blade is a recipe for disaster. Keep those fingers tucked away and slice with confidence. And always remember to give your full attention to the task at hand – no texting while chopping, okay?

Tip #3: Beware of the Heat

Fire up the stove and let's get cookin'! But before you crank up the heat, let's talk about staying safe around those flames. Always use oven mitts or pot holders to handle hot pots and pans, and never leave the stove unattended while it's in use. And if things start to get a little too hot to handle, don't hesitate to ask for help – there's no shame in calling in reinforcements!

Tip #4: Practice Proper

Food Handling Last but not least, let's chat about the importance of handling food with care. From raw meats to fresh veggies, it's crucial to keep everything in its rightful place to prevent cross-contamination. And when it comes to leftovers, don't leave them out on the counter for too long – store them in the fridge promptly to keep them safe and tasty for later.

TOOL TIME: GEAR UP, GET COOKIN'!

Welcome, kitchen warriors! It's time to gear up and get ready to conquer the culinary world with your trusty kitchen tools by your side. In this ultimate guide to kitchen gadgets, we'll explore the must-have equipment that'll take your cooking game to the next level. So grab your apron, tighten your chef's hat, and let's dive into the exciting world of cooking tools!

THE BASICS

Your Starter Kit Every chef needs a solid foundation, and that starts with the basics. Here are the essential tools you'll want to have in your arsenal:

- **Chef's knife:** Your go-to tool for chopping, slicing, and dicing like a pro.

- **Cutting board:** Keep your countertops scratch-free and your veggies in place with a sturdy cutting board.

- **Mixing bowls:** From whisking up batter to tossing salads, a set of mixing bowls will be your best friend in the kitchen.

- **Measuring cups and spoons:** Precision is key when it comes to cooking, so make sure you have a reliable set of measuring tools on hand.

LEVEL UP

Advanced Gadgets for Serious Cooks Ready to take your cooking skills to the next level? These advanced gadgets will help you up your game:

- **Immersion blender:** Say goodbye to lumpy sauces and hello to silky smooth purees with an immersion blender.

- **Instant-read thermometer:** Ensure your meats are cooked to perfection every time with an instant-read thermometer.

- **Mandoline slicer:** Impress your friends with perfectly uniform slices of fruits and veggies courtesy of a mandoline slicer.

- **Stand mixer:** Whip up fluffy cakes and creamy frosting with ease using a stand mixer – perfect for budding bakers!

FUN AND FUNCTIONAL

Specialty Tools for Every Occasion Cooking is all about experimentation, so why not have some fun with specialty tools? Here are a few that'll add some flair to your culinary creations:

- **Spiralizer:** Turn boring veggies into beautiful spirals for colorful salads and pasta dishes.

- **Avocado slicer:** Say goodbye to slippery avocado mishaps with a handy avocado slicer – perfect for avocado toast aficionados.

- **Egg separator:** Get precise separation every time with an egg separator – ideal for recipes that call for egg whites only.

- **Cookie cutters:** Channel your inner artist and create adorable shapes for cookies, sandwiches, and more with a set of cookie cutters.

CARE AND MAINTENANCE

Keeping Your Tools in Top Shape Just like any superhero, your kitchen tools need a little TLC to keep them in top shape. Here are some tips for care and maintenance:

- Clean your tools after each use to prevent food residue from building up.

- Store sharp objects like knives in a safe place to prevent accidents.

- Check for any signs of wear and tear regularly and replace any damaged tools promptly.

FRESH FINDS: PICK 'N' KEEP!

Prepare yourselves for an exciting journey into the realm of fresh ingredients with "Fresh Finds: Pick 'n' Keep!" In this guide, we'll explore everything you need to know about selecting and preserving the freshest ingredients to elevate your culinary creations. So put on your explorer hat and let's dive into the wonderful world of fresh finds!

THE ART OF SELECTION

Choosing the Freshest Ingredients Selecting the right ingredients is the first step to creating mouthwatering dishes that'll impress even the toughest food critics. Here's how to pick the freshest ingredients like a pro:

- **Fruits and Vegetables:** Look for vibrant colors, firm textures, and a fresh aroma. Avoid any signs of bruising, wilting, or mold.

- **Meat and Seafood:** Opt for cuts of meat that are bright red with minimal marbling, and seafood that smells like the ocean – fresh and briny.

- **Dairy and Eggs:** Check for expiration dates and look for dairy products with tight seals and eggs with uncracked shells.

KEEPING IT FRESH

Tips for Proper Storage and Preservation Once you've picked out the perfect ingredients, it's important to store them properly to maintain their freshness and flavor. Here are some tips to keep your ingredients in top condition:

- **Fruits and Vegetables:** Store fruits and veggies in the crisper drawer of your refrigerator, and keep them separate to prevent premature ripening. Use breathable produce bags or paper towels to absorb excess moisture.

- **Meat and Seafood:** Store meat and seafood in the coldest part of your refrigerator or freezer, and use airtight containers or freezer bags to prevent freezer burn. For longer-term storage, consider vacuum-sealing or wrapping in freezer paper.

- **Dairy and Eggs:** Keep dairy products and eggs in their original packaging and store them on the refrigerator shelves, where it's coldest. Avoid storing dairy products in the refrigerator door, as the temperature fluctuates too much.

MAKING THE MOST OF YOUR INGREDIENTS

Creative Ways to Use Fresh Finds Now that you've mastered the art of selecting and preserving fresh ingredients, it's time to get creative in the kitchen! Here are some fun and delicious ways to make the most of your fresh finds:

- **Experiment with different cooking methods:** Try grilling, roasting, sautéing, or steaming your vegetables to bring out their natural flavors.

- **Get adventurous with seasonings and spices:** Mix and match herbs, spices, and marinades to create unique flavor combinations that'll tantalize your taste buds.

- **Incorporate fresh ingredients into your favorite recipes:** Add chopped herbs to salads, sandwiches, and soups, or use fresh fruit as a topping for yogurt, oatmeal, or pancakes.

WASTE NOT, WANT NOT

Tips for Reducing Food Waste As budding chefs, it's important to be mindful of food waste and do our part to minimize it. Here are some tips for reducing food waste in the kitchen:

- Plan your meals ahead of time and make a shopping list to avoid overbuying.

- Get creative with leftovers by incorporating them into new dishes or freezing them for later use.

- Compost food scraps to reduce landfill waste and nourish your garden or houseplants.

COOKIN' LINGO: MASTER THE BASICS!

Hey foodie friends, are you craving some kitchen excitement? Welcome to "Cookin' Lingo: Master the Basics!" Get ready to spice up your culinary skills as we journey through the flavorful world of cooking terminology and essential techniques. So grab your apron and let's whip up some kitchen magic together!

ESSENTIAL SKILLS FOR SUCCESS

Cooking is like a dance – it's all about mastering the steps and finding your rhythm. Here are some fundamental skills to get you groovin' in the kitchen:

- **Chopping and Dicing:** Practice your knife skills and learn how to chop and dice like a pro. Keep those fingers tucked in and let the blade do the work!

- **Sauteing and Stir-Frying:** Master the art of sauteing and stir-frying to create flavorful dishes in a flash. Keep the pan hot and the ingredients moving for even cooking.

- **Baking Basics:** Whether you're whipping up cookies, cakes, or bread, baking is all about precision. Learn how to measure ingredients accurately and follow recipes like a boss.

KITCHEN HACKS AND PRO TIPS

Ready to take your cooking game to the next level? Here are some insider tips to help you cook like a pro:

- Keep a damp cloth under your cutting board to prevent it from slipping while you chop.

- Use the back of a spoon to peel ginger – it's much easier than using a knife!

- To prevent your pasta from sticking together, add a splash of olive oil to the cooking water.

EMBRACING CREATIVITY IN THE KITCHEN

Cooking is an art form, and like any art form, it's all about expressing yourself. Don't be afraid to get creative and put your own spin on recipes. Swap ingredients, experiment with flavors, and don't be afraid to make mistakes – that's how you learn and grow as a chef!

Building Confidence, One Recipe at a Time: Remember, Rome wasn't built in a day, and neither is culinary mastery. Start with simple recipes and gradually work your way up to more complex dishes. With practice and perseverance, you'll soon be whipping up gourmet meals like a pro!

KITCHEN TERMINOLOGY REFERENCE CHART

Term	Definition
Slice	To cut food into thin, flat pieces using a knife or other cutting tool.
Chop	To cut food into small, irregular pieces, typically using a knife.
Dice	To cut food into small, uniform cubes, usually around ¼ to ½ inch in size.
Grate	To shred food into small pieces by rubbing it against a grater or similar tool.
Mix	To combine ingredients together thoroughly, usually by stirring or beating.
Stir	To mix ingredients together gently in a circular motion using a spoon or spatula.
Whisk	To beat ingredients vigorously with a whisk, incorporating air and creating a smooth texture.
Fold	To gently combine ingredients together using a gentle lifting and turning motion, typically done with a spatula.
Sauté	To cook food quickly in a small amount of oil or fat over medium to high heat, stirring frequently.
Simmer	To cook food gently in liquid at a temperature just below boiling, usually for a longer period of time.
Boil	To heat liquid until it reaches its boiling point, causing bubbles to form and rise to the surface.
Bake	To cook food using dry heat in an oven, typically at a specific temperature for a set amount of time.
Broil	To cook food using high heat from above, typically in an oven or under a broiler.
Roast	To cook food using dry heat in an oven, typically at a higher temperature than baking, resulting in a browned exterior.

As you journey into the wonderful world of cooking, remember that every chop, mix, and whisk is like a little dance in the kitchen! With these basic kitchen terms in your recipe book, you're all set to cook up a storm and sprinkle some magic into every dish. So put on your chef's hat, roll up your sleeves, and let's get cooking! Whether you're baking sweet treats, sautéing up savory delights, or simmering a cozy soup, embrace the joy of creating delicious meals that will make your taste buds dance with delight. So go ahead, have fun, and remember that the kitchen is your playground – so get ready to whip up some tasty adventures!

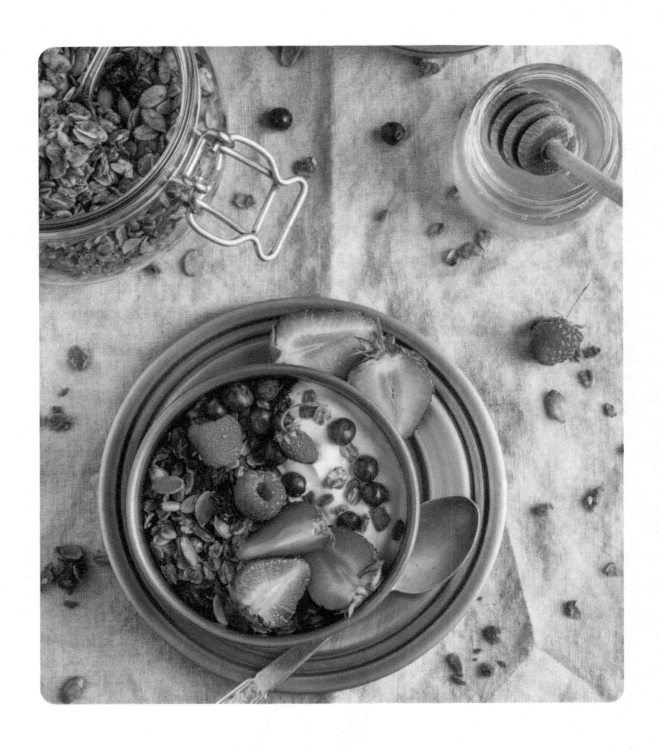

CHAPTER 2: YUMMY BREAKFAST IDEAS

ALMOND-RAISIN GRANOLA

Prep time: **45 minutes** | Cook time: **1 hour 45 minutes** | Serves **5**

- ½ cup flax seeds
- ½ cup sunflower seed kernels
- 1 cup sliced raw almonds
- 3 cups old-fashioned oats
- ¼ cup melted coconut oil
- 1 cup raisins
- 6 tablespoons honey
- 6 tablespoons pure maple syrup
- 2 tablespoons warm water

1. Preheat the oven to 250°F. Line a rimmed baking sheet with parchment paper.
2. In a large mixing bowl, combine the flax seeds, sunflower seed kernels, almonds, and oats.
3. In a separate bowl, whisk together the warm water, melted coconut oil, honey, and maple syrup until smooth.
4. Pour the wet ingredients over the dry ingredients and mix thoroughly to ensure even coating.
5. Spread the mixture in an even layer on the prepared baking sheet.
6. Bake for 1 to 1 ½ hours, stirring occasionally, until the granola is golden brown and crisp.
7. Remove from the oven and let cool completely on the baking sheet.
8. Break into clusters and store in an airtight container for up to 2 weeks.

SWEET SPICY POTATO BREAD

Prep time: **5 minutes** | Cook time: **15 minutes** | Serves **4**

- 4 medium potatoes
- 1 cup buckwheat flour
- ½ teaspoon salt
- ½ teaspoon red chili powder
- ¼ cup honey, for serving

1. Place the potatoes in a large saucepan and cover with water by 1 inch.
2. Bring to a boil, then reduce heat and simmer for 8-10 minutes, or until potatoes are fork-tender.
3. Drain the potatoes and return them to the pot. Mash thoroughly.
4. Add the buckwheat flour, salt, and chili powder to the mashed potatoes. Mix until a smooth dough forms.
5. Divide the dough into 4 equal portions and shape into balls.
6. Using a rolling pin, flatten each ball into a thin disk.
7. Preheat the air fryer to 390°F.
8. Cook the potato breads in the air fryer for 6-7 minutes, or until lightly golden and crisp.
9. Serve warm, drizzled with honey.

BREAD PUDDING WITH APPLES

Prep time: 15 minutes | Cook time: 45 minutes | Serves 6-8

- 8 slices bread, cut into 1-inch cubes
- ¼ cup unsalted butter
- 1 cup hot whole milk
- 1 large apple, peeled, cored, and cubed
- ½ cup raisins
- ½ cup granulated sugar
- ¼ teaspoon salt
- ½ teaspoon ground cinnamon
- ½ teaspoon ground nutmeg
- 2 large eggs, beaten
- ½ cup chopped pecans or walnuts (optional)
- ¾ cup packed brown sugar

1. Preheat the oven to 325°F. Grease a 1 ½-quart casserole dish with butter.
2. Arrange the bread cubes in an even layer in the prepared casserole dish.
3. Melt the butter and stir it into the hot milk. Pour this mixture over the bread cubes and let stand.
4. In a large mixing bowl, combine the cubed apple, raisins, granulated sugar, salt, cinnamon, and nutmeg. Toss to coat evenly.
5. Stir in the beaten eggs and nuts (if using).
6. Pour the fruit mixture over the soaked bread cubes.
7. Sprinkle the brown sugar evenly over the top.
8. Bake on the center oven rack for 45 minutes, or until the pudding is set and the top is golden brown.
9. Let cool for 10 minutes before serving.

HONEYED SEEDS AND OATS GRANOLA

Prep time: 10 minutes | Cook time: 40 minutes | Serves 12

- 2 cups rolled oats
- 2 tablespoons unsalted butter, melted
- 1 cup honey
- ½ teaspoon coconut extract
- ½ teaspoon vanilla extract
- ¼ cup sesame seeds
- ¼ cup pumpkin seeds
- ½ cup unsweetened coconut flakes

1. In a large mixing bowl, combine the oats, melted butter, honey, coconut extract, vanilla extract, sesame seeds, and pumpkin seeds. Mix thoroughly.
2. Preheat the air fryer to 230°F.
3. Spread the mixture evenly in the air fryer basket, using cooking spray if needed to prevent sticking.
4. Cook for 25 minutes, shaking the basket halfway through.
5. Add the coconut flakes and continue cooking for an additional 10-15 minutes, until golden and crisp.
6. Let cool completely before storing in an airtight container for up to 3 weeks.

OLD-FASHIONED WHITE SANDWICH BREAD

Prep time: 30 minutes (plus 1½ hours for dough to rise) | Cook time: **40 minutes** | Makes **2 loaves** (Serves 24)

Equipment:

- Stand mixer or large mixing bowl
- Large bowl
- Plastic wrap
- 2 loaf pans (8 ½ × 4 ½ × 2 ½ inches)
- Pastry brush
- Wire cooling rack

For the Bread:

- 2 cups warm whole milk (105-115°F)
- 2 tablespoons granulated sugar
- 1 (¼-ounce) packet active dry yeast
- 2 tablespoons unsalted butter, room temperature
- 5 to 6 cups all-purpose flour
- 2 teaspoons table salt
- 1 tablespoon vegetable or canola oil

For the Topping:

- 2 tablespoons unsalted butter, melted

1. In the bowl of a stand mixer fitted with the dough hook, combine the warm milk, sugar, and yeast. Let sit for 5 minutes until the mixture becomes foamy.
2. Add the room-temperature butter, 4 cups of flour, and salt to the yeast mixture.
3. Mix on low speed until well blended. Gradually add more flour as needed, a little at a time, until a soft dough forms.
4. Increase mixer speed to medium and knead for 4-6 minutes, until the dough is smooth and elastic.
5. Grease a large bowl with the vegetable oil. Place the dough in the bowl, turning to coat all sides.
6. Cover with plastic wrap and let rise in a warm, draft-free place for 1 hour, or until doubled in size.
7. Punch down the dough and divide it into two equal portions.
8. Shape each portion into a loaf and place in greased 8 ½ × 4 ½ × 2 ½-inch loaf pans.
9. Brush the tops of the loaves with melted butter.
10. Cover and let rise again for 30 minutes.
11. Preheat the oven to 350°F.
12. Bake for 30-40 minutes, or until the loaves are golden brown and sound hollow when tapped.
13. Remove from the oven and let cool in the pans for 5 minutes.
14. Transfer to a wire rack and cool completely before slicing.

CURRIED TUNA MELT ENGLISH MUFFIN

Prep time: **5 minutes** | Cook time: **10 minutes** |Serves **1**

- 2 tablespoons mayonnaise
- ½ teaspoon curry powder
- 1 (3-ounce) can tuna, drained and flaked
- 1 scallion, thinly sliced
- Kosher salt and freshly ground black pepper, to taste
- 1 English muffin, split
- 2 small slices cheddar cheese
- Sweet potato chips, for serving

1. Preheat the broiler and position the oven rack 4-5 inches from the heat source.
2. In a small bowl, mix the mayonnaise and curry powder until well combined.
3. Stir in the flaked tuna and sliced scallion. Season with salt and black pepper to taste.
4. Toast the English muffin halves until lightly golden.
5. Spread the tuna mixture evenly on the cut sides of the English muffin.
6. Top each half with a slice of cheddar cheese.
7. Place the English muffin halves on a baking sheet and broil for 2-3 minutes, or until the cheese is melted and bubbly.
8. Serve immediately, topped with sweet potato chips.

SPRING GREENS & MATZO FRITTATA

Prep time: **50 minutes** | Cooking time: **10 minutes** | Serves **6**

- Nonstick cooking spray
- 1 tablespoon unsalted butter
- 1 bunch thin asparagus (about 1 pound), trimmed and cut into 1-inch lengths
- 5 sheets matzo, broken into large chunks
- 5 large eggs
- 1 cup fresh basil leaves, chopped
- 1 cup frozen peas, thawed
- 1 tablespoon freshly grated lemon zest
- 1 teaspoon kosher salt
- ½ teaspoon freshly ground black pepper

1. Preheat the oven to 350°F. Spray an 8 × 8-inch baking dish with nonstick cooking spray.
2. In a 12-inch skillet over medium heat, melt the butter. Add asparagus and cook for 5-8 minutes, or until crisp-tender. Remove from heat and let cool slightly.
3. In a medium bowl, pour 1 cup warm water over the matzo. Let stand for 5 minutes, or until softened. Drain well and gently squeeze out excess water.
4. In a large bowl, whisk the eggs until well beaten.
5. Stir in the cooled asparagus, softened matzo, basil, peas, lemon zest, salt, and pepper.
6. Pour the mixture into the prepared baking dish.
7. Bake for 40 minutes, or until the top is golden brown and the center is set.
8. Let cool for 10 minutes before serving. Can be made ahead and refrigerated for up to 3 days.

CHOCOLATE-GLAZED BANANA BREAD MINIS

Prep time: 45 minutes | **Cooking time: 15 minutes** | Serves **6**

- 2 cups all-purpose flour
- ¾ teaspoon baking soda
- ¼ teaspoon salt
- 2 cups mashed very ripe bananas (about 4-5 medium bananas)
- 2 teaspoons vanilla extract
- ½ cup (1 stick) unsalted butter, softened
- ½ cup granulated sugar
- ½ cup packed light brown sugar
- 2 large eggs
- 2 ounces semisweet chocolate, melted

1. Preheat the oven to 350°F. Grease six ¼-pound mini loaf pans or line with parchment paper.
2. In a medium bowl, whisk together the flour, baking soda, and salt.
3. In another medium bowl, combine the mashed bananas and vanilla extract.
4. In a large bowl, using an electric mixer, cream the butter and both sugars on medium speed for 3 minutes, or until light and fluffy.
5. Add the eggs one at a time, beating well after each addition.
6. Reduce the mixer speed to low. Alternately add the flour mixture and banana mixture to the butter mixture, beginning and ending with the flour mixture. Mix just until combined, scraping down the sides of the bowl as needed.
7. Divide the batter evenly among the prepared loaf pans.
8. Bake for 30-35 minutes, or until a toothpick inserted into the center of the loaves comes out clean.
9. Cool the loaves completely in the pans on a wire rack.
10. Drizzle melted chocolate over the cooled loaves. Let stand until the chocolate sets.

BASIC OMELET

Prep time: **5 minutes** | Cook time: **10 minutes** | Serves **4**

- 6 large eggs
- ⅓ cup whole milk
- 1 teaspoon kosher salt
- ⅛ teaspoon freshly ground black pepper
- 1 ½ tablespoons unsalted butter

1. In a large mixing bowl, beat the eggs using an electric hand mixer on high speed (or whisk vigorously by hand) until the yolks and whites are well blended.
2. Add the milk, salt, and pepper. Beat thoroughly to combine.
3. Heat a medium skillet over medium-high heat. Melt the butter, tilting the pan to coat the bottom and sides completely.
4. Reduce the heat to low and pour in the egg mixture.
5. As the eggs begin to set, use a spatula to lift the edges, allowing uncooked egg to flow underneath.
6. Continue cooking and lifting the edges for about 10 minutes, until the eggs are fully set and golden brown on the bottom.
7. Using the spatula, loosen the omelet from the pan.
8. Fold the omelet in half by tilting the pan and sliding it onto a plate.

OATMEAL-RAISIN MUFFINS

Prep time: **35 minutes** | Cooking time: **15 minutes** | Serves **12**

- 2 ½ cups all-purpose flour
- ½ cup granulated sugar
- 1 tablespoon baking powder
- ½ teaspoon salt
- 1 cup whole milk
- 6 tablespoons unsalted butter, melted
- 1 teaspoon vanilla extract
- 1 large egg
- 1 cup old-fashioned or quick-cooking oats
- ½ cup raisins

1. Preheat the oven to 400°F. Grease a 12-cup muffin pan or line with paper liners.
2. In a large bowl, whisk together the flour, sugar, baking powder, and salt.
3. In a separate bowl, whisk together the milk, melted butter, vanilla extract, and egg until well blended.
4. Pour the wet ingredients into the dry ingredients and stir just until the flour is evenly moistened. Do not overmix.
5. Gently fold in the oats and raisins.
6. Divide the batter evenly among the prepared muffin cups.
7. Bake for 18-20 minutes, or until a toothpick inserted into the center of a muffin comes out clean.
8. Remove the muffins from the oven and let cool in the pan for 5 minutes.
9. Transfer to a wire rack to cool completely, or serve warm.

JALAPEÑO CHEESE TWISTS

Prep time: 5 minutes | Cook time: 1 hour |Serves 24

- 1 cup finely grated Parmesan cheese (about 4 ounces)
- 1 1/3 cups shredded sharp cheddar cheese (about 4 ounces)
- 4 tablespoons (½ stick) unsalted butter, at room temperature
- 1 ¾ cups all-purpose flour, plus more for rolling
- 1 ½ teaspoons kosher salt
- ½ teaspoon freshly ground black pepper
- 1 jalapeño pepper, halved, seeded, and finely minced
- ¼ cup plus 1 tablespoon heavy cream

1. Line two baking sheets with parchment paper.
2. In a food processor, combine the Parmesan, cheddar, butter, flour, salt, black pepper, and minced jalapeño. Pulse in 5-second bursts until the mixture resembles coarse sand, with a few pea-sized pieces of butter visible (about 45 seconds).
3. Drizzle in the cream and process until the dough forms a ball (about 15 seconds).
4. On a lightly floured surface, roll the dough into a 14-inch square, about 1/8 inch thick.
5. Cut the dough in half to create two 7 × 14-inch rectangles. Cut each rectangle crosswise into ½-inch wide strips (you'll have about 50 strips).
6. Gently twist each strip into a spiral. Place on prepared baking sheets, leaving ½ inch between twists.
7. Press the ends of the strips against the baking sheets to help them hold their shape.
8. Refrigerate the twists for at least 20 minutes (or up to 3 days if covered with plastic wrap).
9. Preheat the oven to 400°F.
10. Bake for 15 minutes, or until the twists are firm and golden brown.
11. Let the twists rest on the baking sheets for 5 minutes, then transfer to a wire rack to cool completely.
12. Store in an airtight container at room temperature for up to 1 week.

CHAPTER 3: TASTY LUNCH ADVENTURES

CHEESY EGG SANDWICH

Prep time: 5 minutes | Cook time: 10 minutes | Serves 4

- Olive oil
- 1 baguette or crusty bread
- ⅔ cup grated sharp cheddar cheese
- 4 large eggs
- 4 handfuls of greens (arugula or spinach), rinsed and patted dry
- Sea salt
- Freshly ground black pepper

Equipment:

- Bread knife
- Box grater
- Toaster oven
- Small cast-iron skillet
- Metal spatula

1. Slice the baguette into 5-inch sections and split horizontally.
2. Drizzle olive oil on the cut sides of the bread.
3. Toast in the toaster oven until golden and crispy, about 3 minutes.
4. Sprinkle cheese evenly over the toast.
5. Broil until the cheese is melted and bubbly, about 5 minutes.
6. In a small cast-iron skillet, heat a thin layer of olive oil over medium-high heat.
7. Crack the eggs into the skillet. Cook for 1 minute on high heat, then reduce to medium heat.
8. Cook until the whites are set but the yolks remain soft.
9. Season the eggs with salt and pepper.
10. Assemble the sandwiches: Place greens on the bottom half of the bread, top with a fried egg, and cover with the cheesy toast.
11. Serve immediately, with a plate underneath to catch any runny yolk.

POTATO MIXED GREEN ROLL

Prep time: 10 minutes | Cook time: 13 minutes | Serves 2

- ½ pound russet potatoes
- 1 teaspoon olive oil
- ½ teaspoon minced garlic
- 2 cups loosely packed mixed greens, torn into pieces
- 2 tablespoons oat milk
- Sea salt and freshly ground black pepper, to taste
- ¼ teaspoon crushed red pepper flakes
- Nonstick cooking spray
- Tomato ketchup (optional, for serving)

1. Boil the potatoes for 30 minutes, or until fork-tender.
2. Drain and peel the potatoes. Place in a mixing bowl and mash thoroughly.
3. Stir in olive oil, garlic, mixed greens, oat milk, salt, black pepper, and red pepper flakes.
4. Shape the mixture into bite-sized balls.
5. Preheat the air fryer to 390°F.
6. Lightly spray the potato balls with nonstick cooking spray.
7. Place the balls in the air fryer basket and cook for 13 minutes, shaking the basket halfway through.
8. Serve hot with tomato ketchup, if desired.

CHICKEN BREAST WITH OLIVE TAPENADE

Prep time: 5 minutes | Cook time: 10 minutes | Serves 1

- 1 boneless, skinless chicken breast
- 3 garlic cloves
- ½ cup olive tapenade
- 2 tablespoons coconut oil
- Salt and pepper to taste

1. Slice the chicken breast into 3 thin cutlets.
2. Peel the garlic cloves and gently crush with the flat side of a knife.
3. Heat coconut oil in a skillet over medium heat.
4. Add the crushed garlic cloves and sauté for 2 minutes.
5. Add the chicken cutlets to the skillet.
6. Cook for 3-4 minutes on each side, or until the chicken is golden brown and cooked through.
7. Top the chicken with olive tapenade before serving.

SUBMARINE SANDWICH

Prep time: 5 minutes | Cook time: 5 minutes | Serves 1

- 1 submarine roll (also called a hoagie roll)
- 2 tablespoons mayonnaise
- ½ teaspoon salt
- ½ teaspoon freshly ground black pepper
- 2 tablespoons Italian dressing
- 2 slices (4 ounces total) ham
- 2 slices (4 ounces total) salami
- 4 slices Swiss cheese
- 1 medium tomato, sliced
- ½ cup shredded lettuce

1. Split the submarine roll in half lengthwise.
2. Spread 1 tablespoon of mayonnaise on each half of the roll. Tip: You can add other condiments like mustard if you prefer.
3. Sprinkle salt and pepper over the bread, then drizzle with Italian dressing.
4. Layer the ham, salami, and cheese on the bottom half of the roll.
5. Top with tomato slices and shredded lettuce.
6. Close the sandwich and enjoy!

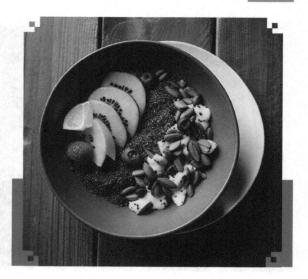

PAN GRAVY

Prep time: **5 minutes** | Cook time: **10 minutes** | Serves **4-6**

- 1 cup all-purpose flour
- 1 cup water
- Pan drippings from roasted turkey
- Salt to taste
- Freshly ground black pepper to taste

1. In a small mixing bowl, whisk the flour and water together until smooth, making sure there are no lumps.
2. In a large saucepan over medium-high heat, bring the turkey drippings to a simmer for about 4 minutes.
3. Slowly pour in the flour mixture, whisking continuously to prevent lumps from forming.
4. Continue cooking and whisking until the gravy reaches your desired thickness and turns a golden color.
5. Taste the gravy and season with salt and pepper as needed.
6. Serve hot.

FRUITY-NUTTY BREAKFAST BOWL

Prep time: **10 minutes** | Cook time: **none** | Serves **4**

- 2 cups Greek yogurt
- 4 tablespoons ground flaxseed
- 2 tablespoons chia seeds
- 4 tablespoons peanut butter
- 3 cups mixed fresh fruit (such as pomegranate seeds, blueberries, raspberries, chopped apples, persimmon, or pears)
- ½ cup unsweetened coconut flakes, toasted
- 2 tablespoons mixed nuts (almonds or pistachios), toasted and coarsely chopped

Equipment:

- Toaster oven (optional, for toasting coconut and nuts)

1. Stir the yogurt until smooth and creamy.
2. Divide the yogurt evenly among four bowls.
3. Sprinkle ground flaxseed and chia seeds evenly over the yogurt.
4. Add a dollop of peanut butter on top of each bowl.
5. Top with mixed fresh fruit.
6. Scatter toasted coconut flakes and chopped nuts over each bowl.
7. Serve and enjoy immediately.

CHINESE MEATBALL SLIDERS WITH PINEAPPLE SALAD

Prep time: 10 minutes | **Cook time: 30 minutes** | Serves **4**

For the Meatballs:

- Cooking spray
- 2 tablespoons hoisin sauce
- 2 tablespoons plus 1 teaspoon rice vinegar (unseasoned)
- 12 ounces ground pork
- 2 tablespoons panko breadcrumbs
- 1 scallion, white and light green parts only, finely chopped
- 1 teaspoon grated fresh ginger
- Kosher salt
- Freshly ground black pepper
- 12 mini potato slider buns
- Shredded romaine lettuce for topping

For the Pineapple Salad:

- ¼ small head green cabbage, chopped
- 2 small carrots, chopped
- ½ cup chopped fresh pineapple
- 1 tablespoon mayonnaise, plus extra for buns

1. Preheat the oven to 425°F. Place a rack in the upper third of the oven.
2. Spray a rimmed baking sheet with cooking spray.
3. In a small bowl, mix 1 tablespoon hoisin sauce and 1 teaspoon rice vinegar; set aside.
4. In a medium bowl, combine ground pork, panko, remaining hoisin sauce, scallion, ginger, ½ teaspoon salt, and a few grinds of black pepper. Mix thoroughly with your hands.
5. Roll the mixture into twelve 1 ½-inch meatballs and place on the prepared baking sheet.
6. Bake for 5-6 minutes, then carefully turn the meatballs using tongs. Bake for an additional 5-6 minutes until browned and cooked through.
7. Brush the cooked meatballs with the reserved hoisin sauce mixture.
8. For the pineapple salad, combine cabbage, carrots, pineapple, remaining rice vinegar, mayonnaise, and ½ teaspoon salt in a food processor. Pulse until vegetables are roughly chopped.
9. Spread mayonnaise on the bottom of each slider bun.
10. Top with shredded lettuce and a meatball.
11. Serve with pineapple salad on the side.

EVERYTHING BAGEL PIZZA-TASTIC RINGS

Prep time: 35 minutes | Cooking time: 30 minutes | Serves 5

- 3 tablespoons sesame seeds
- 3 tablespoons poppy seeds
- 3 tablespoons dried onion flakes
- 1 tablespoon coarse salt
- 4 ounces Pizza-Tastic Dough (per ring)

1. Preheat the oven to 425°F.
2. Line a large rimmed baking sheet with parchment paper.
3. In a shallow dish, mix sesame seeds, poppy seeds, dried onion flakes, and coarse salt.
4. For each bagel ring, roll 4 ounces of Pizza-Tastic Dough into a 10-inch rope.
5. Pinch the ends of the rope together to form a ring.
6. Bring a large pot of water to a boil.
7. Carefully boil each dough ring for 2 minutes, turning occasionally.
8. Using a slotted spoon, transfer the rings to the seed mixture and coat thoroughly.
9. Place the coated rings on the prepared baking sheet.
10. Bake for 25 minutes or until deep golden brown.
11. Serve warm or toasted.

CORNED BEEF HASH

Prep time: 10 minutes | Cook time: 15 minutes | Serves 4

- 2 cups chopped cooked corned beef
- 1 small onion, diced
- 1 pound radishes, diced
- 2 cloves garlic, minced
- ½ cup beef broth
- 1 tablespoon cooking oil
- Salt and pepper to taste

1. Heat 1 tablespoon of oil in a large skillet over medium-high heat.
2. Add the diced onions and sauté for 3-4 minutes until softened.
3. Stir in the diced radishes and continue to cook for 5 minutes.
4. Add the minced garlic and sauté for an additional 1 minute.
5. Pour in the beef broth and simmer for 5 minutes, or until the radishes are tender and the liquid has reduced.
6. Stir in the chopped corned beef and season with salt and pepper.
7. Cook for another 2-3 minutes until everything is heated through and well combined.
8. Taste and adjust seasoning if needed.
9. Serve hot and enjoy your delicious corned beef hash!

BEET, APPLE AND WATERCRESS SALAD

**Prep time: 15 minutes | Cook time: 1 hour |
Serves 6**

- 1 bunch golden beets (about 1 pound), trimmed
- 1 Granny Smith apple, unpeeled, cored and diced
- 1 bunch watercress, trimmed
- 3 tablespoons red wine vinegar
- 1 tablespoon olive oil
- ¼ teaspoon salt
- ⅛ teaspoon black pepper

1. Preheat the oven to 400°F.
2. Wrap beets in aluminum foil and roast for 1 hour.
3. Remove beets from oven and let cool until comfortable to handle.
4. Peel the beets by gently rubbing off the skin, then dice.
5. In a salad bowl, combine the diced beets, apple, and watercress.
6. In a small bowl, whisk together the red wine vinegar, olive oil, salt, and pepper.
7. Drizzle the dressing over the salad and toss gently to coat evenly.
8. Serve immediately.

SAUSAGE-AND-PEPPER DOGS

**Prep time: 5 minutes | Cook time: 20 minutes
|Serves 4**

- 4 hot dogs
- 2 tablespoons extra-virgin olive oil
- 2 bell peppers (any color), sliced
- 1 onion, sliced
- 1 clove garlic, finely chopped
- Pinch of cayenne pepper
- Pinch of fennel seeds
- 4 hoagie rolls, split open

1. Using a sharp knife, carefully cut the hot dogs in half lengthwise.
2. Heat olive oil in a medium skillet over medium heat.
3. Add the hot dogs, bell peppers, and onion. Cook, stirring occasionally, until the hot dogs are warmed through and the vegetables are tender, 5 to 7 minutes.
4. Add the garlic, cayenne pepper, and fennel seeds. Stir in a splash of water and cook for an additional minute.
5. Meanwhile, toast the hoagie rolls in a toaster oven or under the broiler.
6. Using tongs, pile the hot dogs, peppers, and onions onto the toasted hoagie rolls.
7. Serve immediately.

CHAPTER 4: FUN DINNER CREATIONS

GOLDEN BUTTERY DROP BISCUITS

Prep time: 10 minutes | Cook time: 12 minutes | Serves 12

- 2 cups all-purpose flour
- 1 tablespoon baking powder
- 2 tablespoons white sugar
- ½ tablespoon cream of tartar
- ¼ tablespoon salt
- ½ cup butter, melted
- 1 cup milk

1. Preheat the oven to 450°F.
2. In a large mixing bowl, whisk together flour, baking powder, sugar, cream of tartar, and salt.
3. Stir in the melted butter and milk until the mixture is just combined. Be careful not to overmix.
4. Using a tablespoon, drop the batter onto a greased baking sheet, leaving space between each biscuit.
5. Bake for 12 minutes or until the biscuits are golden brown.
6. Serve warm and enjoy!

SPICY BEEF AVOCADO CUPS

Prep time: 5 minutes | Cook time: 15 minutes | Serves 2

- 1 beef steak, cut into small cubes
- 2 chili peppers, chopped
- ½ medium onion, diced
- 2 tablespoons avocado oil
- 2 tablespoons gluten-free tamari sauce or coconut aminos
- 1 large ripe avocado, halved

1. Heat avocado oil in a skillet over high heat.
2. Cook the beef cubes to your preferred doneness.
3. Add chopped peppers and onions to the skillet. Cook until softened.
4. Add more avocado oil if needed.
5. Return the beef to the skillet and season with tamari sauce.
6. Spoon the beef mixture into avocado halves and serve.

MINTY LAMB BURGERS

Prep time: 10 minutes | **Cook time:12–15 minutes** | Serves **4**

- 1 ½ pounds ground lamb
- 1 garlic clove, finely grated
- 3 tablespoons fresh mint, finely chopped
- 3 tablespoons fresh parsley, finely chopped
- ½ teaspoon cumin seeds, toasted and ground
- Kosher salt
- Freshly ground black pepper
- Olive oil, for brushing
- Ciabatta rolls
- Easy Tzatziki
- Romaine lettuce leaves

Optional Toppings:
- Feta cheese, thinly sliced
- Red onion, thinly sliced

Equipment:
- Fine grater
- Medium mixing bowl
- Pastry brush
- Grill pan
- Tongs
- Bread knife

1. In a medium bowl, gently mix the ground lamb with grated garlic, chopped mint, chopped parsley, ground cumin, and a pinch each of salt and pepper.
2. Divide the meat into 4 equal patties, each about ½ inch thick, and place on a plate.
3. Use your fingers to press a small dimple in the center of each patty to prevent bulging during cooking.
4. Lightly brush the patties with olive oil and season again with salt and pepper.
5. Heat the grill pan over high heat. Lightly brush the grate with olive oil.
6. Grill the patties over medium heat:
   - 7-8 minutes for medium-rare
   - 8-10 minutes for medium
7. Turn the patties halfway through cooking.
8. Transfer the patties to a plate to rest.
9. Slice the ciabatta rolls horizontally and brush lightly with olive oil.
10. Grill the rolls cut-side down until lightly charred, 3-5 minutes.
11. Assemble by placing the burgers on the grilled rolls.
12. Top with Easy Tzatziki, romaine lettuce, and optional toppings.

EASY GROUND BEEF TACOS

Prep time: 5 minutes | Cook time: 15 minutes | Makes 4 tacos

- ⅓ pound ground beef
- 3 tablespoons tomato sauce
- 1 tablespoon water
- 4 hard taco shells or 6-inch soft corn tortillas

Taco Seasoning:

- 1 teaspoon chili powder
- 1 teaspoon all-purpose flour
- ½ teaspoon ground cumin
- ¼ teaspoon salt
- ¼ teaspoon dried oregano
- ¼ teaspoon garlic powder
- ¼ teaspoon ground black pepper

Optional Toppings:

- Shredded Cheddar cheese
- Chopped tomatoes
- Shredded lettuce
- Sour cream
- Guacamole

1. In a small bowl, mix all the taco seasoning ingredients together.
2. Heat a skillet over medium-high heat and add the ground beef.
3. Break up the beef with a spoon as it cooks.
4. Sprinkle the seasoning mixture over the beef and cook for about 5 minutes, until the beef is no longer pink.
5. Reduce heat to medium. Stir in tomato sauce and water.
6. Cook for 7 minutes, stirring occasionally, until the sauce thickens slightly.
7. Warm the taco shells according to package directions.
8. Spoon about 2 heaping tablespoons of taco meat into each shell.
9. Add desired toppings and serve.

CREAMY CHICKEN AND BROCCOLI CASSEROLE

Prep time: 5 minutes | **Cook time: 45 minutes** | Serves **6**

- 6 chicken breasts
- 4 cups chicken broth
- 1 (10.75-ounce) can cream of celery soup
- 1 (10.75-ounce) can cream of chicken soup
- 1 (8-ounce) package herb-seasoned breadcrumbs, divided
- ½ cup butter, melted
- 1 (12-ounce) bag frozen broccoli florets, thawed and drained

1. In a large saucepan over high heat, combine the chicken breasts and chicken broth. Add enough water to cover the chicken by ½ inch. Reduce the heat to low as the liquid begins to boil, and simmer for 15 minutes, or until the internal temperature of the chicken reaches 165°F.
2. Transfer the chicken to a plate and let it rest for 5 minutes. Then, chop the chicken into 1-inch cubes. Save the cooking broth.
3. Preheat the oven to 350°F. Grease a 13x9-inch baking dish.
4. In a medium mixing bowl, combine the cream of celery and cream of chicken soups with 2 cups of the reserved broth. Whisk until smooth.
5. In a small bowl, mix ¾ cup of breadcrumbs with the melted butter until the breadcrumbs are evenly coated.
6. Spread the buttered breadcrumbs along the bottom of the prepared baking dish. Top with chicken chunks and broccoli florets. Pour the soup mixture over the top and sprinkle the remaining dry breadcrumbs over the casserole.
7. Bake uncovered on the center rack for 45 minutes, or until bubbly and golden brown.

SUMMERY CORN AND WATERMELON SALAD

Prep time: 15 minutes | **Cook time: 5 minutes** | Serves **4**

- 5 fresh basil leaves
- ½ small watermelon, seeded, rind removed, cut into 1-inch cubes
- 2 ears fresh sweet corn, cooked and kernels removed
- 1 teaspoon ground sumac
- ¼ teaspoon ground cayenne
- Zest of ½ lemon
- Flake salt (such as Maldon)

Equipment:

- Zester

1. Transfer the cubed watermelon and its juices to a serving platter.
2. Add the corn kernels, leaving some rows intact for texture.
3. Just before serving, sprinkle sumac and cayenne over the mixture.
4. Add lemon zest.
5. Prepare basil chiffonade:
   - Stack basil leaves
   - Roll into a tight bundle
   - Slice across the roll to create thin strips
6. Separate and scatter basil strips over the salad.
7. Season with flake salt and serve immediately.

CHAPTER 4

ONE-POT ZUCCHINI MUSHROOM PASTA

Prep time: 10 minutes | **Cook time: 10 minutes** | **Serves 4-6**

- 1 pound pasta
- 2 zucchinis, thinly sliced
- 1 pound cremini mushrooms, thinly sliced
- 2/3 cup frozen peas
- 2 garlic cloves, minced
- ½ teaspoon dried thyme
- 4 ½ cups water
- ¼ cup heavy cream
- ½ teaspoon salt
- ¼ teaspoon freshly ground black pepper
- ⅓ cup grated Parmesan cheese

1. In a large pot, combine the pasta, zucchini, mushrooms, peas, garlic, thyme, and water.
2. Bring to a boil over medium-high heat. Reduce the heat to medium-low and simmer, uncovered, for 10 minutes, or until the pasta is al dente.
3. Drain any excess water from the pot.
4. Stir in the cream, salt, pepper, and Parmesan cheese. Mix well and serve hot.

TORTELLINI & SPINACH SOUP

Prep time: 5 minutes | **Cook time: 15 minutes** | **Serves 6**

- 2 tablespoons olive oil
- 6 garlic cloves, minced
- 6 cups chicken broth
- 20 ounces packaged fresh cheese tortellini
- 1 (14.5-ounce) can crushed tomatoes
- 12 ounces baby spinach leaves
- Salt (to taste)
- Freshly ground black pepper (to taste)

Tools & Equipment
- Cutting board
- Knife
- Large pot
- Wooden spoon
- Ladle

1. In a large pot over medium-high heat, heat the olive oil. Add the garlic and sauté for 30 seconds.
2. Pour in the chicken broth and increase the heat to high. Bring to a boil.
3. Once the broth is boiling, add the tortellini and cook for half the time recommended on the package.
4. Add the crushed tomatoes, reduce the heat to medium-low, and continue cooking until the tortellini is tender.
5. Stir in the spinach and cook until it wilts, about 1 minute.
6. Season with salt and pepper to taste. Ladle into bowls and serve hot.

RIGATONI BOLOGNESE

Prep time: 5 minutes | Cook time: 30 minutes |Serves 4

- Kosher salt
- 12 ounces rigatoni
- 1 (28-ounce) can whole peeled tomatoes
- 4 garlic cloves (2 whole, 2 sliced)
- Freshly ground black pepper
- 2 tablespoons extra-virgin olive oil
- 1 pound ground beef
- ¼ cup red wine or low-sodium beef or chicken broth

1. Fill a large pot with water and season generously with salt. Bring to a boil over high heat.
2. Add the rigatoni and cook according to package directions for al dente pasta.
3. Carefully remove ½ cup of pasta cooking water using a liquid measuring cup; set aside.
4. Drain the rigatoni in a colander, then set aside.
5. In a food processor, combine the whole peeled tomatoes, 2 whole garlic cloves, ½ teaspoon salt, and ½ teaspoon black pepper. Purée until smooth; set aside.
6. Heat olive oil in a large saucepan over medium-high heat. Add the 2 sliced garlic cloves and cook, stirring, for 1 minute.
7. Add the ground beef and cook, breaking up the meat with a wooden spoon, until browned, about 5 minutes.
8. Carefully pour out all but about 1 tablespoon of the drippings from the pan.
9. Add the wine or broth to the saucepan and cook until the pan is dry, about 3 minutes.
10. Stir in the tomato purée. Reduce heat to medium and simmer, stirring occasionally, until thickened, about 20 minutes. Season with additional salt and pepper to taste.
11. Add the rigatoni to the sauce and toss to coat, adding reserved cooking water as needed to loosen the sauce.
12. Serve hot in bowls.

ROASTED BRUSSELS SPROUTS AND SHALLOTS

Prep time: **10 minutes** | Cook time:**30 minutes** | Serves **4**

- 1 ½ pounds Brussels sprouts, trimmed and halved
- 6 shallots, quartered
- 3 tablespoons olive oil
- Salt (to taste)
- Freshly ground black pepper (to taste)
- 1 lemon, cut into wedges (for serving)

Tools & Equipment

- 2 baking sheets
- Tongs

1. Position one oven rack in the top third of the oven and another in the bottom third. Preheat the oven to 450°F.
2. Divide the Brussels sprouts and shallots between two baking sheets. Drizzle with olive oil, making sure to place most of the Brussels sprouts cut-side down. Season generously with salt and pepper.
3. Roast the vegetables, swapping the pan positions halfway through cooking. Use tongs to turn the vegetables for even roasting.
4. Continue roasting until the vegetables are caramelized and tender, about 25 to 30 minutes.
5. Transfer the roasted Brussels sprouts and shallots to a serving dish. Serve with lemon wedges on the side for squeezing.

GRAINY MUSTARD-POTATO SALAD

Prep time: **10 minutes** | Cook time:**10 minutes** | Serves **4**

- 6 medium Yukon Gold potatoes, scrubbed and cut into chunky wedges
- 3 medium Red Bliss potatoes, scrubbed and cut into chunky wedges
- 4 to 5 tablespoons olive oil
- 2 tablespoons whole-grain mustard
- 1 tablespoon capers, rinsed and chopped
- 1 shallot, thinly sliced
- 3 tablespoons fresh dill, torn into small sprigs
- Salt (to taste)
- Freshly ground black pepper (to taste)

Tools & Equipment

- Large saucepan
- Colander
- Large bowl

1. Place potatoes in a large saucepan and cover with water. Gently boil for 8 to 10 minutes, or until fork-tender.
2. Drain the potatoes in a colander and transfer to a large bowl.
3. In the same bowl, toss the potatoes with olive oil, mustard, capers, and sliced shallot.
4. Allow the potato mixture to cool to room temperature. Add dill sprigs and toss again.
5. Season with salt and pepper to taste.
6. Serve warm, at room temperature, or chilled.

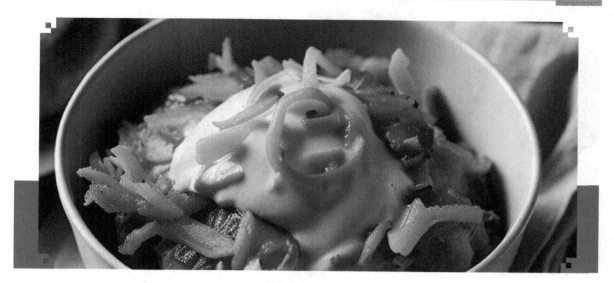

CREAMY PORK CHOP CASSEROLE

Prep time: 10 minutes | **Cook time: 55 minutes** | Serves **6**

- 1 tablespoon vegetable oil
- 6 pork chops (½ to ¾ inch thick)
- Salt (to taste)
- 1 (10.75-ounce) can condensed cream of celery soup
- ½ cup milk
- ½ cup sour cream
- ¼ teaspoon freshly ground black pepper
- 1 (24-ounce) bag frozen hash brown potatoes, thawed
- 1 cup shredded cheddar cheese, divided
- 1 (2.8-ounce) can French fried onions

1. Preheat the oven to 350°F.
2. Heat vegetable oil in a large skillet over medium heat. Add pork chops and cook for 6 minutes on each side, or until golden brown. Drain and discard the oil. Sprinkle the chops with a pinch of salt.
3. In a large bowl, mix the cream of celery soup, milk, sour cream, pepper, and ½ teaspoon salt. Stir in the thawed hash brown potatoes, ½ cup of cheese, and ½ can of French fried onions.
4. Spread the potato mixture in a 9x13-inch baking dish. Arrange the pork chops on top.
5. Cover the casserole and bake on the center rack for 35 minutes, or until the pork chops are cooked through and the mixture is bubbling.
6. Remove the cover and top with the remaining ½ cup of cheese and remaining French fried onions.
7. Bake uncovered for an additional 5 minutes, or until the onions are golden brown.

CHAPTER 5: SNACK
TIME FUN

GREEK YOGURT PARFAIT

Prep time: 5 minutes | **Cook time: 5 minutes** | Serves **2**

- 1 cup Greek yogurt
- ½ cup granola
- ½ cup mixed fresh berries (strawberries, blueberries, raspberries)
- 1 tablespoon honey (optional)
- Fresh mint leaves for garnish (optional)

1. In a glass or bowl, create layers starting with Greek yogurt, then granola, and mixed berries.
2. Repeat the layering process until all ingredients are used or the container is filled.
3. If desired, drizzle honey over the top.
4. Garnish with fresh mint leaves.
5. Serve immediately and enjoy this refreshing and nutritious snack!

ZUCCHINI FRIES

Prep time: 10 minutes | **Cook time: 20 minutes** | Serves **2**

- Nonstick cooking spray
- 1 teaspoon Italian seasoning
- ½ cup grated Parmesan cheese
- 1 cup panko breadcrumbs
- 4 zucchinis, quartered lengthwise
- ½ cup all-purpose flour
- 2 large eggs, beaten
- 2 tablespoons fresh parsley, chopped

1. Preheat the oven to 425°F. Spray an ovenproof cooling rack with nonstick cooking spray and place it on a baking sheet.
2. In a medium mixing bowl, combine Italian seasoning, Parmesan cheese, and panko breadcrumbs.
3. Prepare the zucchini: First coat the zucchini quarters in flour, then dip in beaten eggs, and finally coat with the seasoned breadcrumb mixture.
4. Arrange the coated zucchini on the prepared baking rack.
5. Bake for about 20 minutes, or until golden and crispy.
6. Garnish with chopped parsley before serving.

CRANBERRY BRIE TWISTS

Prep time: 35 minutes | Cooking time: 25 minutes | Serves 12

- ⅓ cup dried cranberries
- 2 tablespoons cran-raspberry juice
- ½ teaspoon grated lemon zest
- ¼ teaspoon salt
- 1 pound Brie cheese
- 1 sheet puff pastry, thawed
- Kitchen string (for tying)

1. Preheat the oven to 400°F. Line a 15½ x 10½-inch rimmed baking sheet with parchment paper.
2. In a small bowl, combine dried cranberries, cran-raspberry juice, lemon zest, and salt.
3. Roll out the puff pastry into a 14-inch square. Place the entire Brie wheel in the center of the pastry.
4. Cut off and discard the top rind of the Brie. Spread the cranberry mixture over the top of the cheese.
5. Carefully gather the pastry around the Brie, twisting the center to create a decorative seal. Use kitchen string to secure the twist and trim any excess dough.
6. Bake for 25 minutes, or until the pastry is golden brown and puffy.

NO-BAKE ENERGY BITES

Prep time: 5 minutes | Cook time: 30 minutes |Serves 5

- 1 cup rolled oats
- ½ cup peanut butter (or almond butter)
- ⅓ cup honey
- ½ cup mini chocolate chips
- ¼ cup ground flaxseed (optional)
- 1 teaspoon vanilla extract

1. In a large mixing bowl, combine all ingredients: rolled oats, peanut butter, honey, chocolate chips, flaxseed (if using), and vanilla extract.
2. Stir until all ingredients are thoroughly mixed.
3. Using clean hands, roll the mixture into small balls, about 1 inch in diameter.
4. Place the energy bites on a parchment-lined baking sheet.
5. Refrigerate for at least 30 minutes to firm up.
6. Store in an airtight container in the refrigerator for up to one week.

RAINBOW SUGAR COOKIES

Prep time: 1 hour | **Cooking time: 30 minutes** | Serves **36**

For the Cookies

- 2 cups all-purpose flour
- ½ teaspoon baking soda
- ¼ teaspoon salt
- ¾ cup (1½ sticks) butter, softened
- 1 cup granulated sugar
- 2 large eggs
- ½ cup low-fat buttermilk

For the Icing

- 1 package (16 ounces) confectioners' sugar
- 2 tablespoons light corn syrup
- 2 tablespoons milk
- ⅛ teaspoon salt
- Assorted food coloring

1. Position oven racks in the top and bottom thirds of the oven. Preheat to 350°F. Line two large cookie sheets with parchment paper.
2. In a medium bowl, whisk together flour, baking soda, and salt.
3. In a large bowl, use an electric mixer to beat butter and granulated sugar for 3 minutes until fluffy. Add eggs one at a time, beating well after each addition.
4. Reduce mixer speed to low. Alternately add flour mixture and buttermilk, beginning and ending with flour mixture. Mix just until blended.
5. Drop dough by rounded tablespoonfuls onto prepared cookie sheets, spacing 2 inches apart.
6. Bake for 13 to 15 minutes, rotating cookie sheets between racks halfway through, until golden brown.
7. Transfer cookies to wire racks and cool completely.
8. For the icing, beat confectioners' sugar, corn syrup, milk, and salt in a large bowl until smooth.
9. Divide icing and tint with food coloring as desired. Spread icing on flat sides of cooled cookies.
10. Let icing set for 30 minutes before serving.

AIR FRIED GARLIC SPICED ALMOND

Prep time: **10 minutes** | Cook time: **6 minutes** | Serves **6**

- 1½ cups raw almonds
- Sea salt (to taste)
- Ground black pepper (to taste)
- ¼ teaspoon garlic powder
- ¼ teaspoon mustard powder
- ½ teaspoon cumin powder
- ¼ teaspoon smoked paprika
- 1 tablespoon olive oil

1. In a mixing bowl, toss almonds with olive oil and all spices until evenly coated.
2. Line the air fryer basket with parchment paper.
3. Spread almonds in a single layer in the basket. Work in batches if necessary to avoid overcrowding.
4. Air fry at 350°F for 6 to 8 minutes, shaking the basket once or twice during cooking.
5. Let cool slightly before serving.

TAHINI AND APRICOT OAT BARS

Prep time: **5 minutes** | Cook time: **35 minutes** |Serves **6**

- Nonstick cooking spray
- 2¼ cups rolled oats
- 7 tablespoons unsalted butter
- ¼ cup packed light brown sugar
- ½ cup sweetened condensed milk
- ⅓ cup tahini
- 2 tablespoons honey
- ½ cup chopped dried apricots
- ⅔ cup chopped pecans
- 3 tablespoons sesame seeds or flaxseeds

1. Preheat the oven to 350°F. Line an 8-inch square baking pan with parchment paper, leaving overhang on two sides for easy removal. Spray the pan and parchment with cooking spray.
2. Place oats in a large bowl. In a medium saucepan, combine butter, brown sugar, and condensed milk. Cook over medium heat, stirring until smooth and sugar dissolves, about 3 minutes.
3. Remove from heat and stir in tahini and honey. Pour over oats and mix until thick and sticky.
4. Fold in dried apricots, pecans, and sesame seeds.
5. Spread mixture evenly in the prepared pan.
6. Bake for 15 to 20 minutes, until golden on top.
7. Let bars rest in the pan for 30 minutes. Use parchment to lift out and transfer to a wire rack to cool completely.
8. Slice into 10 bars. Store in an airtight container for up to 1 week.

BEST-EVER BUTTERMILK BISCUITS

Prep time: 25 minutes | Cook time: 15 minutes | Makes 14 biscuits

- 4 cups all-purpose flour
- 5 teaspoons baking powder
- 1 tablespoon sugar
- 1 teaspoon baking soda
- ¾ teaspoon salt
- ½ cup vegetable shortening, cold and cut into small pieces
- 1½ cups low-fat buttermilk
- 3 tablespoons unsalted butter, melted

1. Preheat the oven to 450°F. Line a large baking sheet with parchment paper.
2. In a food processor with the blade attachment, pulse together flour, baking powder, sugar, baking soda, and salt until combined. Add the shortening and pulse just until coarse crumbs form. Transfer the mixture to a large bowl.
3. Stir in buttermilk just until the dough begins to come together. Do not overmix.
4. Turn the dough onto a lightly floured surface. Knead gently just until smooth, about 6 to 8 times. Using a floured rolling pin, roll the dough to ½-inch thickness.
5. Using a floured 2½-inch round biscuit cutter, cut out biscuit rounds. Press straight down without twisting the cutter. Carefully transfer the rounds to the prepared baking sheet, spacing them 1 inch apart.
6. Gather the dough scraps, gently press together, and reroll. Cut additional biscuits. You should have about 14 total.
7. Brush the tops of the biscuits with melted butter. Bake for 12 to 15 minutes, or until golden brown. Serve warm.

COOKIE DOUGH BITES

Prep time: 45 minutes | Cook time: 30 minutes | Makes 18-20 bites

- 6 ounces mini chocolate chips
- 2 cups all-purpose flour
- 1 teaspoon vanilla extract
- 1½ cups light brown sugar
- 1 cup (2 sticks) unsalted butter, softened

1. In a large mixing bowl, cream together butter and sugar until smooth.
2. Add remaining ingredients and mix thoroughly. (Using clean hands can help mix the ingredients more evenly.)
3. Roll the mixture into 1-inch balls.
4. Place the balls on a parchment-lined baking sheet. Refrigerate for 30 minutes.
5. Optional: Drizzle or dip balls in melted chocolate.
6. Before serving, let the bites sit at room temperature for 10 minutes.
7. Store leftover bites in an airtight container in the refrigerator.

GLUTEN-FREE PEANUT BUTTER COOKIES

Prep time: 15 minutes | Cook time: 20 minutes | Makes 16-18 cookies

- 2 cups creamy peanut butter (not natural)
- 1½ cups packed light brown sugar
- ½ teaspoon baking soda
- ½ teaspoon kosher salt
- 2 large eggs
- 2 teaspoons pure vanilla extract

1. In a stand mixer with the paddle attachment, beat peanut butter, brown sugar, baking soda, and salt on medium speed until smooth, about 3 minutes.
2. Add eggs one at a time, beating well after each addition. Mix in vanilla extract.
3. Chill the dough in the refrigerator for 30 minutes.
4. Preheat the oven to 350°F. Line two baking sheets with parchment paper.
5. Shape dough into 1½-tablespoon balls. Place on prepared baking sheets, spacing 2 inches apart.
6. Using a fork, gently press a crisscross pattern onto the top of each cookie.
7. Bake, rotating pans halfway through, for about 15 minutes or until edges are golden and tops are slightly crinkled.
8. Let cookies cool on baking sheets for 10 minutes, then transfer to a wire rack to cool completely.
9. Store in an airtight container for up to 5 days.

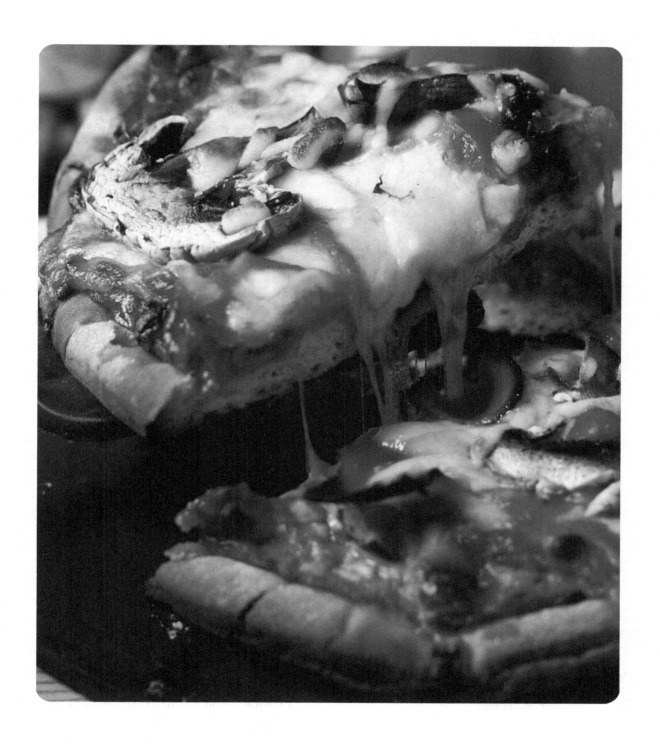

CHAPTER 6: PIE, PIZZA, AND TART TIME

PITTA PIZZA

Prep time: 10 minutes | Cook time: 10 minutes | Serves 4

- 4 whole-wheat pita breads
- 4 tablespoons sun-dried tomato paste
- 3 ripe plum tomatoes, thinly sliced
- 1 small shallot, thinly sliced
- 3 ounces diced chorizo
- ½ cup shredded cheddar cheese
- Fresh basil leaves (optional)

1. Preheat the oven to 400°F. Place a baking sheet in the oven to heat up.
2. Spread 1 tablespoon of sun-dried tomato paste on each pita bread.
3. Top with sliced plum tomatoes, shallot, diced chorizo, and shredded cheddar cheese.
4. Carefully transfer the prepared pitas to the hot baking sheet. Bake for 10 minutes or until the cheese is melted and bubbly.
5. If desired, scatter fresh basil leaves on top. Serve hot and enjoy!

MINI S'MORES PIE

Prep time: 15 minutes | Cook time: 15 minutes | Makes 6 mini pies

- 1 premade pie crust
- 2 graham crackers
- 6 marshmallows
- 1 milk chocolate bar
- Cooking spray

1. Preheat oven to 375°F.
2. Lightly grease a muffin pan with cooking spray.
3. Unroll the premade pie crust and cut out 3-inch rounds.
4. Place one crust round in each muffin cup, pressing to fit.
5. Crush graham crackers and divide crumbs evenly among the muffin cups.
6. Break the chocolate bar into small rectangles. Place two rectangles and one marshmallow in each cup.
7. Bake for 15 minutes, or until crust is golden and marshmallows are lightly toasted.
8. Let cool for a few minutes before serving.

MINI ORANGE COOKIE TARTS

Prep time: 30 minutes (plus 30 minutes chill time) | **Cook time: 25 minutes** | Makes **20 tarts**

For the Crust:

- ½ cup (1 stick) unsalted butter, softened
- ½ cup powdered sugar
- 1 cup all-purpose flour
- ⅛ teaspoon salt

For the Filling:

- ½ cup plus 2 tablespoons sweetened condensed milk
- ¼ cup freshly squeezed orange juice (from 1-2 oranges)
- 2 tablespoons orange zest
- 2 large egg yolks
- ½ teaspoon orange extract
- ¼ teaspoon vanilla extract

Equipment:

- 2 medium mixing bowls
- Electric hand mixer
- Whisk
- Zester
- 24-cup mini muffin pan

1. Preheat the oven to 325°F.
2. In a medium bowl, beat the butter with an electric mixer on medium speed for about 10 seconds, until smooth.
3. Add powdered sugar and beat until light and fluffy, about 2 minutes.
4. Gradually mix in the flour and salt until just combined.
5. In another bowl, whisk together condensed milk, orange juice, orange zest, egg yolks, orange extract, and vanilla extract until well blended.
6. Grease a 24-cup mini muffin pan. Press a rounded teaspoon of cookie dough into about 20 cups, pushing the dough up the sides to form little cups.
7. Spoon about 2 teaspoons of filling into each cookie cup, filling each to about ¾ full.
8. Bake for 20 to 25 minutes, or until the filling is set and the cookies are golden brown.
9. Cool slightly in the pan, then transfer to the refrigerator to chill for about 30 minutes.

MOROCCAN PIZZA

Prep time: 25 minutes | Cooking time: 15 minutes | Serves 6

- 4 pitas (5-6 inches)
- 2 teaspoons olive oil
- 2 cups shredded rotisserie chicken
- 1 cup marinara sauce
- ½ teaspoon ground cumin
- ¼ teaspoon ground cinnamon
- ¼ teaspoon ground black pepper
- ½ cup shredded carrots
- ¼ cup sliced green olives
- 1 cup shredded part-skim mozzarella cheese
- 2 green onions, thinly sliced (for garnish)

1. Preheat oven to 450°F. Line a large baking sheet with aluminum foil.
2. Arrange pitas on the prepared baking sheet in a single layer. Brush each pita lightly with olive oil.
3. In a large bowl, mix chicken, marinara sauce, cumin, cinnamon, and black pepper until evenly coated.
4. Divide the chicken mixture evenly among the pitas.
5. Top with shredded carrots, sliced olives, and mozzarella cheese.
6. Bake for 10 to 15 minutes, or until cheese is melted and pita edges are crisp.
7. Garnish with sliced green onions before serving.

PIZZA POCKETS

Prep time: 10 minutes | Cook time: 35 minutes | Makes 12 pockets

- 1 pound pizza dough, at room temperature
- All-purpose flour (for dusting)
- 2 tablespoons tomato sauce
- ¼ cup shredded mozzarella cheese
- 2 tablespoons grated Parmesan cheese
- 1 large egg, beaten
- 1 cup broccoli florets

1. Preheat the oven to 400°F.
2. Place broccoli in a microwave-safe bowl. Add 1 tablespoon water, cover, and microwave until tender and bright green, about 2 minutes. Drain and set aside.
3. On a lightly floured surface, roll out the pizza dough to ¼-inch thickness.
4. Cut the dough into twelve 3-inch rounds using a cookie cutter or small glass.
5. Spoon a small amount of tomato sauce, broccoli, mozzarella, and Parmesan onto each dough round, leaving a small border.
6. Brush the edges with beaten egg. Fold each round in half and press edges with your fingers or a fork to seal.
7. Line a baking sheet with parchment paper. Place the pockets on the sheet.
8. Brush the tops with remaining beaten egg and sprinkle with additional Parmesan.
9. Poke a small hole in the top of each pocket with a skewer.
10. Bake for 20-25 minutes, or until golden brown. Let cool slightly before serving.

RASPBERRY SWIRL CHEESECAKE PIE

Prep time: 30 minutes | **Cook time: 55 minutes** | **Serves 6-8**

- 1 unbaked 9-inch pie crust
- 2 (8-ounce) packages cream cheese, softened
- ½ cup granulated sugar
- ½ teaspoon vanilla extract
- 2 large eggs
- 3 tablespoons raspberry jam

1. Preheat oven to 450°F. Line unbaked pie shell with double-thickness heavy-duty foil.
2. Bake for 5 minutes. Remove foil and bake for an additional 5 minutes.
3. Reduce oven temperature to 350°F.
4. In a large mixing bowl, beat cream cheese, sugar, and vanilla until smooth.
5. Add eggs, mixing on low speed until just blended.
6. Pour filling into the prepared pie crust.
7. Drizzle raspberry jam over the top. Use a knife to create swirl patterns by gently cutting through the filling.
8. Bake for 25-30 minutes, or until the center is almost set.
9. Cool on a wire rack for 1 hour.
10. Refrigerate overnight.
11. Before serving, let stand at room temperature for 30 minutes.

PUFF PASTRY PLUM TART WITH ALLSPICE AND HONEY

Prep time: 5 minutes | **Cook time: 40 minutes** | **Serves 8**

- ½ teaspoon ground allspice
- ¼ teaspoon freshly ground black pepper
- ⅛ teaspoon kosher salt
- All-purpose flour (for rolling)
- 1¼ pounds black plums (6-7 medium), halved, pitted, and sliced ½-inch thick
- 1 (10-inch) sheet all-butter puff pastry, thawed
- 2 tablespoons honey (for serving)

1. Preheat oven to 425°F. Line a baking sheet with parchment paper.
2. In a small bowl, mix allspice, black pepper, and salt. Set aside.
3. On a lightly floured surface, roll the puff pastry into a 10 x 12-inch rectangle. Transfer to the prepared baking sheet.
4. Dock the pastry by pricking it with a fork, leaving a ¾-inch border around the edges untouched.
5. Arrange plum slices in overlapping rows inside the border. Sprinkle evenly with the spice mixture.
6. Bake for 25 minutes, or until pastry is puffed and golden and plums are tender.
7. Cool on the pan for 15 minutes. Transfer to a cutting board and slice into 8 rectangles.
8. Drizzle with honey before serving.

CHAPTER 6

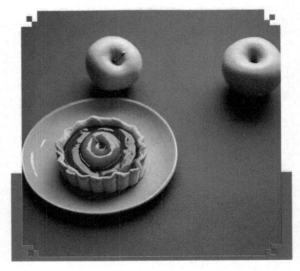

TOMATO SPINACH PIE

Prep time: **10 minutes** | Cook time: **40 minutes** | Serves **8-10**

- 1 unbaked pie crust
- 1½ cups shredded mozzarella cheese, divided
- 5 Roma or medium tomatoes
- 1 cup baby spinach leaves
- 1 teaspoon minced garlic
- ½ cup mayonnaise
- ¼ cup grated Parmesan cheese
- ⅛ teaspoon freshly ground black pepper

1. Bake the pie crust according to package directions. Immediately sprinkle with ½ cup mozzarella cheese.
2. Adjust oven temperature to 375°F. Slice tomatoes and drain on paper towels to remove excess moisture.
3. Arrange tomato slices over the cheese. Chop spinach and distribute over tomatoes.
4. In a medium bowl, combine garlic, remaining mozzarella, mayonnaise, Parmesan, and black pepper.
5. Spread the cheese mixture evenly over the spinach and tomatoes.
6. Bake for 35 minutes, or until the top is golden and bubbly.
7. Serve warm.

CARAMEL APPLE TART

Prep time: **5 minutes** | Cook time: **35 minutes** | Serves **4**

- 1 sheet frozen puff pastry, thawed
- 5 medium Granny Smith apples, peeled and cored
- 2 tablespoons unsalted butter
- 16 soft caramel candies, unwrapped
- ½ teaspoon ground cinnamon

1. Preheat oven to 425°F. Line a baking sheet with parchment paper.
2. Place puff pastry on the prepared pan. Gently roll to smooth out any creases. Prick the pastry all over with a fork.
3. Bake for 15 minutes, or until golden brown. Set aside.
4. Cut each apple into 8 wedges. In a large skillet over medium heat, melt the butter.
5. Add apple wedges and cook for 10 minutes, stirring occasionally, until they begin to soften.
6. Reduce heat to low and cook for an additional 5 minutes, until apples are tender.
7. Remove apples and set aside. In the same skillet, add caramels and cinnamon over low heat.
8. Cook for 5 minutes, stirring frequently, until caramels are melted.
9. Return apples to the skillet and gently fold to coat with caramel.
10. Spoon the caramel apples over the prepared pastry and serve warm.

44

ZUCCHINI-PESTO PIZZA

Prep time: 30 minutes | Cooking time: 10 minutes | Serves 4

- 2 small tomatoes
- ¼ teaspoon kosher salt
- ½ cup store-bought refrigerated pesto
- 8 ounces zucchini and/or summer squash
- 2 teaspoons olive oil
- ⅓ cup grated Pecorino cheese
- ¼ teaspoon freshly ground black pepper
- Zest of 1 small lemon
- ¼ cup fresh mint leaves
- 1 pre-made pizza dough (12-inch)

1. Place a rack in the center of the oven and preheat to 450°F. If you have a pizza stone, place it in the oven while preheating.
2. Thinly slice the tomatoes and sprinkle with salt. Let sit for 10 minutes to draw out excess moisture.
3. Stretch or roll out the pizza dough on a piece of parchment paper. Spread the pesto evenly over the dough, leaving a ½-inch border around the edges.
4. Using a mandoline or sharp knife, carefully slice the zucchini and/or summer squash lengthwise into thin rounds.
5. In a medium bowl, toss the zucchini and squash slices with olive oil until evenly coated.
6. Arrange the salted tomato slices and oiled zucchini/squash slices over the pesto-covered dough.
7. Sprinkle the grated Pecorino cheese and black pepper evenly over the vegetables.
8. Using a vegetable peeler, carefully remove long strips of lemon zest and scatter over the pizza.
9. Slide the pizza (with the parchment paper) onto the hot pizza stone or a preheated baking sheet.
10. Bake for 8-10 minutes, or until the crust is golden and the vegetables are lightly roasted.
11. Remove from the oven and let cool for 2-3 minutes.
12. Tear fresh mint leaves and sprinkle over the pizza just before serving.
13. Slice into wedges and serve immediately.

CHAPTER 7: COOL ICE CREAMS AND DRINKS

HOMEMADE STRAWBERRY ICE CREAM

Prep time: 20 minutes | Cook time: 10 minutes | Serves 2

- 6 large egg yolks
- 2 cups whole milk
- 1 cup granulated sugar
- ¼ teaspoon kosher salt
- 1 teaspoon pure vanilla extract
- 2 cups heavy whipping cream
- 2 cups fresh strawberries, hulled and crushed
- 2 tablespoons granulated sugar (for strawberries)

1. In a medium saucepan, whisk together egg yolks, milk, 1 cup sugar, and salt.
2. Create a double boiler by placing the saucepan over a pot of simmering water. Cook, stirring constantly, until the mixture thickens and coats the back of a spoon (about 10-12 minutes).
3. Remove from heat and strain the custard through a fine-mesh sieve into a clean bowl. Let cool to room temperature, stirring occasionally.
4. In a separate bowl, mix crushed strawberries with 2 tablespoons sugar. Let sit for 15 minutes to release juices.
5. Stir the vanilla extract and heavy cream into the cooled custard.
6. Fold in the macerated strawberries.
7. Pour the mixture into an ice cream maker and churn according to manufacturer's instructions.
8. Transfer to a freezer-safe container and freeze for 2-4 hours before serving.

FRUITY GRANITA DELIGHT

Prep time: 5 minutes | Cook time: 10 minutes | Freeze time: 2½ hours |Serves 4

- 3 cups strawberries or pineapple, chopped
- 2 tablespoons granulated sugar
- 2 tablespoons honey
- 1 tablespoon fresh lemon juice
- 3 cups ice cubes, divided

1. In a food processor or blender, combine fruit, sugar, honey, lemon juice, and 2 cups of ice. Pulse until chunky.
2. Add the remaining 1 cup of ice and blend until smooth.
3. Pour the mixture into a 9x13-inch baking dish.
4. Freeze for 30 minutes, then use a fork to scrape and break up the ice crystals.
5. Return to the freezer and continue freezing for 2-2.5 hours, scraping with a fork every 30 minutes to create a slushy texture.
6. Serve immediately in chilled glasses.

COCONUT ICE POPS

Prep time: **10 minutes** | Freeze time: **4 hours** | Serves **4 to 8**

- 3 (5.4-ounce) cans unsweetened organic coconut cream
- Juice and zest of 1 lime
- ⅓ cup maple syrup or honey

Equipment
- Zester
- Food processor or blender
- Rubber spatula
- Ice pop molds or small paper cups
- Wooden ice pop sticks
- Clothespins or binder clips

1. In a food processor, purée the coconut cream, lime zest, lime juice, and maple syrup until smooth.
2. Pour the mixture into ice pop molds or small paper cups, leaving about ¼ inch of space at the top.
3. Insert wooden ice pop sticks. If using molds, use clothespins or binder clips to hold sticks in place and prevent them from sinking.
4. Freeze for at least 4 hours, or until completely solid.
5. To unmold, either:
   - Briefly run molds under warm water
   - Peel away paper cups

CHOCOLATE FROSTING

Prep time: **10 minutes** | Cook time: **20 minutes** | Frosts **12 Cupcakes**

- 2 tablespoons unsalted butter, softened
- 1 tablespoon unsweetened cocoa powder
- 10 tablespoons powdered sugar
- ⅛ teaspoon pure vanilla extract
- ½ to 1 tablespoon whole milk

1. In a medium mixing bowl, cream the softened butter and cocoa powder until well combined.
2. Gradually add powdered sugar, 2 tablespoons at a time, mixing thoroughly after each addition.
3. Stir in vanilla extract.
4. Slowly add milk, ½ tablespoon at a time, mixing until the frosting reaches a smooth, spreadable consistency.
5. If the frosting is too thick, add a little more milk. If too thin, add more powdered sugar.
6. Use immediately by spreading on cooled cakes or cupcakes, or transfer to a piping bag for decorative application.

VANILLA MILKSHAKES

Prep time: 5 minutes | **Cook time: 20 minutes** | **Serves 2 to 4 (Makes about 3 cups)**

- 4 cups vanilla ice cream
- ½ cup whole milk
- Pinch of salt

Tools

- 2 to 4 glasses
- Food processor
- Rubber spatula

1. Place glasses in the freezer to chill for 10-15 minutes before serving.
2. Remove ice cream from the freezer and let it soften at room temperature for about 15 minutes.
3. Add the softened ice cream, milk, and salt to the food processor. Secure the lid.
4. Pulse the mixture for 30 seconds. Stop and use the rubber spatula to scrape down the sides of the bowl.
5. Process again until smooth, about 30 seconds more. (Ask an adult to help you remove the processor blade safely.)
6. Pour the milkshakes into the chilled glasses and serve immediately.

BANANA "ICE CREAM"

Prep time: 7 minutes1 hour to freeze | **Cook time: none** | **Serves 4**

- 5-8 ripe but firm bananas
- Pinch of kosher salt

Optional Mix-Ins

- Fresh berries
- Greek yogurt or crème fraîche
- Ground cinnamon
- Nut butters
- Chocolate chips

Tools

- Baking sheet
- Food processor
- Rubber spatula

1. Peel the bananas and cut them into ½-inch thick coins.
2. Spread the banana coins on a baking sheet and freeze for 1 to 2 hours (or overnight).
3. Add the frozen banana coins and a pinch of salt to the food processor.
4. Blend until smooth and creamy, about 5 minutes. Stop periodically to scrape down the sides of the bowl.
5. Watch the bananas magically transform into "ice cream"! If desired, add mix-ins and pulse to combine.
6. For the best texture, let the "ice cream" sit at room temperature for 10 minutes before serving.
7. Store leftovers in a covered container in the freezer for up to 5 days.

CHERRY ALMOND ICE CREAM

Prep time: 1 hour 15 minutes | Cook time: 10 minutes | Serves 4

- 2 cups heavy cream
- ½ cup granulated sugar
- 1 cup pitted cherries
- 1 tablespoon lemon juice
- 1 ½ teaspoons almond extract
- ¼ cup slivered almonds

Tools

- Blender
- Ice cream maker

1. Purée the cherries in a blender until smooth.
2. In a large bowl, combine the puréed cherries, cream, sugar, lemon juice, and almond extract. Stir until the sugar dissolves completely.
3. Gently fold in the slivered almonds.
4. Pour the mixture into an ice cream maker and freeze according to the manufacturer's instructions.

WATERMELON-LIME SORBET

Prep time: 10 minutes, plus 6 hours to freeze | Cook time: 5 minute | Serves 6

- 6 cups cubed watermelon
- ¼ cup water
- 3 tablespoons granulated sugar
- ¼ cup freshly squeezed lime juice (from 2 to 3 limes)

Tools

- Baking sheet
- Parchment paper
- Small saucepan
- Food processor or high-powered blender

1. Line a baking sheet with parchment paper. Spread the watermelon cubes in a single layer and freeze for 30 minutes.
2. Transfer the partially frozen watermelon to a freezer-safe container and freeze for at least 6 hours or overnight.
3. To make the simple syrup, combine water and sugar in a small saucepan. Heat over medium heat, stirring until the sugar completely dissolves. Remove from heat and let cool slightly.
4. Add the frozen watermelon and lime juice to a food processor or blender.
5. Drizzle in the warm simple syrup and blend until the mixture becomes an icy slush.
6. Serve immediately or freeze for an additional 30 minutes for a firmer texture.

EASY VANILLA ICE CREAM

Prep time: **5 minutes** | Cook time: **15 minutes** | Freeze time: **24 hours** | Serves **6**

- 2 cups heavy cream
- 1 cup whole milk
- 1/3 cup granulated sugar
- 1 tablespoon pure vanilla extract
- ¼ cup light corn syrup
- ¼ teaspoon kosher salt

Tools

- Medium saucepan
- Medium bowl
- Whisk
- Ice cream maker

1. In a medium saucepan, combine cream, milk, sugar, vanilla, corn syrup, and salt.
2. Heat over medium heat, stirring occasionally, until the mixture is warm and the sugar has dissolved (about 3 minutes). To check, stir and taste a small spoonful - it should be smooth with no sugar granules.
3. Pour the ice cream base into a medium bowl, cover, and refrigerate until completely chilled, at least 5 hours or up to 2 days.
4. Transfer the chilled base to an ice cream maker and churn according to the manufacturer's instructions.
5. For soft-serve, enjoy immediately. For a firmer texture, transfer to an airtight container and freeze for at least 6 hours or overnight.

UNICORN FROSTING

Prep time: **10 minutes** | Cook time: **20 minutes** | Serves **12**

- 6 tablespoons powdered sugar
- 2 tablespoons unsalted butter, softened
- ½ tablespoon heavy whipping cream
- ⅛ teaspoon vanilla extract
- Food coloring (3 different colors)
- Edible glitter (optional)

Tools

- Mixing bowl
- Whisk or electric mixer
- Small bowls for coloring
- Spatula

1. In a mixing bowl, combine the softened butter and powdered sugar. Beat with a whisk or electric mixer until the mixture is well combined and creamy.
2. Gradually add the whipping cream, about ½ tablespoon at a time, mixing well after each addition. The frosting should be smooth and spreadable.
3. Stir in the vanilla extract and mix until the frosting is fluffy and light.
4. Divide the frosting evenly into three small bowls.
5. Add a few drops of different food coloring to each bowl. Mix thoroughly until you achieve your desired vibrant colors.
6. Use the frosting immediately by spreading it onto baked goods or transferring to piping bags for decorating cupcakes or cakes.
7. For an extra magical touch, sprinkle edible glitter over the frosted treats.

FROZEN YOGURT BANANA POPS

Prep time: **5 minutes** | Freeze time: **3 hours 10 minutes** | Serves **8**

- 2 ripe bananas
- 1 cup strawberry yogurt

Toppings (choose 1-2):
- Sliced almonds
- Granola
- Shredded coconut
- Crushed freeze-dried strawberries

Tools
- Cutting board
- Chef's knife
- Baking sheet
- Parchment paper
- Wooden popsicle sticks

1. Line a baking sheet with parchment paper.
2. Cut each banana in half crosswise, then cut each half lengthwise, creating 4 total banana pieces.
3. Insert a wooden popsicle stick into the bottom of each banana piece.
4. Place the banana pops on the prepared baking sheet and freeze until completely firm, about 3 hours.
5. Pour the strawberry yogurt into a tall glass or narrow container for easy dipping.
6. Remove frozen bananas from the freezer. Quickly dip each banana into the yogurt, coating all sides.
7. Immediately sprinkle with your chosen toppings. Work quickly so the yogurt doesn't melt.
8. Return the topped banana pops to the baking sheet and freeze for an additional 10 minutes until set.

FROZEN LIMEADE

Prep time: 5 minutes | Freeze time: 2-3 hours | Serves 4 to 6 (Makes about 6 cups)

- 7 limes
- 1 cup granulated sugar

- 4½ cups cold water

Tools

- Cutting board
- Chef's knife
- Large bowl
- Potato masher
- Citrus juicer
- Rubber spatula

- Fine-mesh strainer
- Large pitcher
- 2 ice cube trays
- Blender
- Dish towel
- Serving glasses

1. Prepare the lime slices: Cut one lime in half through both ends. Place the halves flat-side down on the cutting board and slice each half into thin semicircles.
2. In a large bowl, combine the lime slices and sugar. Use a potato masher to press and mix until the sugar is completely moistened, about 1 minute.
3. Cut the remaining 6 limes in half crosswise. Use a citrus juicer to squeeze all the juice into the bowl with the sugar and lime slices.
4. Pour the cold water into the bowl. Use a rubber spatula to stir until the sugar completely dissolves, about 1 minute.
5. Place a fine-mesh strainer over a large pitcher. Carefully pour the mixture through the strainer, using the spatula to press and extract as much juice as possible from the lime slices. Discard the used lime slices.
6. Pour half of the lime mixture into two ice cube trays. Freeze until solid, 2 to 3 hours. Refrigerate the remaining lime juice mixture.
7. Once the lime juice cubes are frozen, remove them from the trays and add to the blender.
8. Pour the remaining refrigerated lime juice over the frozen cubes.
9. Secure the blender lid and hold it in place with a folded dish towel. Blend until smooth, 30 to 60 seconds.
10. Pour immediately into glasses and serve.

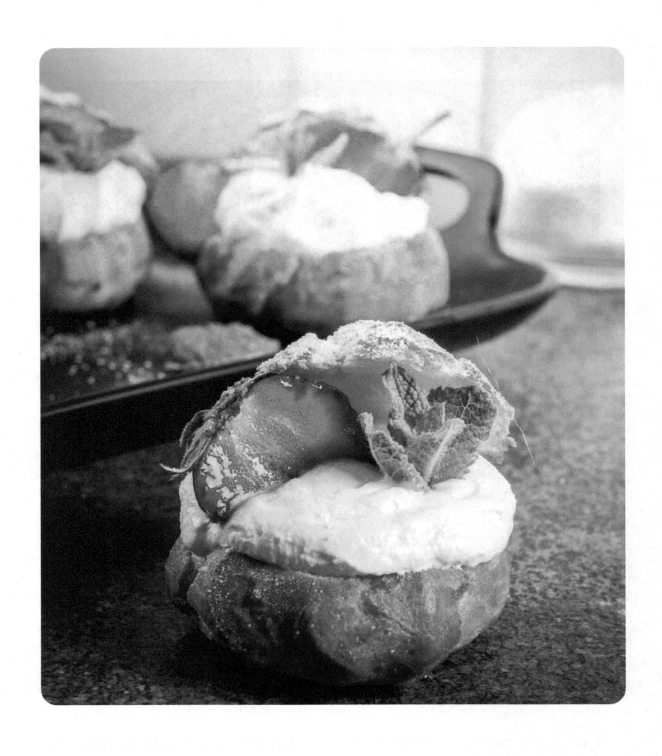

CHAPTER 8: SWEET TREATS GALORE

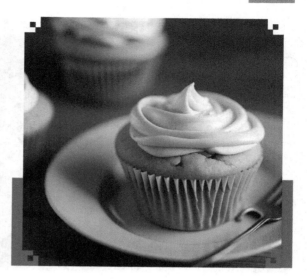

EVE'S PUDDING

Prep time: 30 minutes | **Cook time: 45 minutes** | **Serves 6**

- 14 tablespoons unsalted butter, divided
- 6 Granny Smith apples
- 1 cup raisins
- ½ cup brown sugar
- 4 large eggs
- 1 ½ cups self-rising flour

Special Equipment

- 9x13-inch baking dish

1. Preheat the oven to 350°F. Grease a 9x13-inch baking dish with 3 tablespoons of butter.
2. Peel, core, and slice the Granny Smith apples. Arrange the slices evenly in the greased baking dish.
3. Sprinkle raisins evenly over the apple slices.
4. In a large mixing bowl, cream together the remaining 11 tablespoons of butter and brown sugar until light and fluffy.
5. Beat in the eggs one at a time, mixing well after each addition.
6. Gently fold in the self-rising flour until the batter is just combined and smooth.
7. Carefully spread the batter evenly over the apples and raisins.
8. Bake for 45-50 minutes, or until the top is golden brown and a toothpick inserted into the center comes out clean.
9. Serve warm with a scoop of vanilla ice cream or custard.

GOLDEN BUTTER CUPCAKES

Prep time: 35 minutes | **Cooking time: 25 minutes** | **Serves 24**

- 2 cups all-purpose flour
- 1 ½ cups granulated sugar
- 2 ½ teaspoons baking powder
- 1 teaspoon salt
- ¾ cup (1 ½ sticks) unsalted butter, softened
- ¾ cup whole milk
- 1 ½ teaspoons vanilla extract
- 3 large eggs

1. Preheat oven to 350°F. Line 24 muffin cups with paper liners.
2. In a large bowl, combine flour, sugar, baking powder, and salt on low speed until mixed.
3. Add softened butter, milk, vanilla extract, and eggs. Beat on low speed until ingredients are just blended.
4. Increase mixer speed to high and beat for 1-2 minutes until the batter is creamy and smooth. Occasionally scrape down the sides of the bowl.
5. Spoon batter evenly into prepared muffin cups, filling each about 2/3 full.
6. Bake for 20-25 minutes, or until cupcakes are golden brown and a toothpick inserted in the center comes out clean.
7. Immediately remove cupcakes from the pan and cool completely on a wire rack.
8. Once cooled, frost as desired.

YUMMY CHOCOLATE CAKE

Prep time: 30 minutes | Cook time: 55 minutes | Serves 16

- 1 package chocolate cake mix
- 1 package (2.1 oz) sugar-free instant chocolate pudding mix
- 1 ¾ cups water
- 3 egg whites

Frosting

- 1 ¼ cups cold fat-free milk
- ¼ teaspoon almond extract
- 1 package (1.4 oz) sugar-free instant chocolate pudding mix
- 1 carton (8 oz) frozen reduced-fat whipped topping, thawed
- Chocolate curls (optional)

Special Equipment

- 15x10x1-inch baking pan

1. Preheat oven to 350°F. Grease a 15x10x1-inch baking pan with cooking spray.
2. In a large bowl, combine egg whites, water, pudding mix, and cake mix.
3. Beat on low speed for 60 seconds, then increase to medium speed and beat for 2 additional minutes.
4. Pour batter into the prepared baking pan.
5. Bake for 12-18 minutes, or until a toothpick inserted in the center comes out clean.
6. Cool completely on a wire rack.

For the Frosting

7. In a large bowl, combine milk and almond extract.
8. Gradually add pudding mix, stirring for 2 minutes after each addition.
9. Let the mixture stand for 15 minutes.
10. Gently fold in the whipped topping.
11. Frost the cooled cake and garnish with chocolate curls if desired.

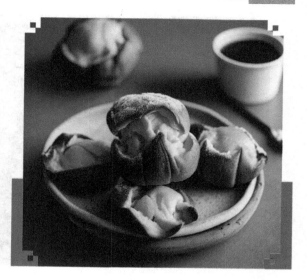

VEGAN BROWNIES

Prep time: 10 minutes | Cook time: 30 minutes | Serves 12

- 2 cups all-purpose flour
- 2 cups white sugar
- ¾ cup unsweetened cocoa powder
- 1 teaspoon baking powder
- 1 teaspoon salt
- 1 cup water
- 1 cup vegetable oil
- 1 teaspoon vanilla extract

1. Preheat oven to 350°F. Grease a 9x13-inch baking pan.
2. In a large bowl, whisk together flour, salt, baking powder, sugar, and cocoa powder.
3. Add vanilla extract, vegetable oil, and water. Mix until the batter is smooth and well combined.
4. Spread the batter evenly in the prepared baking pan.
5. Bake for 30 minutes, or until a toothpick inserted in the center comes out with just a few moist crumbs.
6. Remove from oven and let cool completely on a wire rack.
7. Cut into squares and serve.

CLASSIC POPOVERS

Prep time: 10 minutes | Cook time: 50 minutes | Serves 6

- 3 large eggs
- 1 cup whole milk
- 1 cup all-purpose flour
- 3 tablespoons unsalted butter, melted, plus more for greasing
- ½ teaspoon salt

1. Preheat oven to 375°F. Generously grease a popover pan with butter.
2. In a blender, combine eggs, milk, flour, melted butter, and salt. Blend until smooth.
3. Divide batter evenly among the prepared popover cups.
4. Bake for 40 minutes, then quickly cut a small slit in the top of each popover to release steam.
5. Bake for an additional 10 minutes until deep golden brown.
6. Remove from oven and immediately transfer popovers to a wire rack.
7. Serve warm.

APRICOT-ALMOND SKILLET CAKE

Prep time: 5 minutes | Cook time: 1 hours |Serves 8

- Nonstick pan spray
- 1 ¼ cups all-purpose flour
- 1 teaspoon baking powder
- ¾ teaspoon ground cardamom, divided
- ½ teaspoon kosher salt
- 1 stick (4 ounces) unsalted butter, room temperature
- ¾ cup granulated sugar
- 2 large eggs
- 2 teaspoons pure almond extract
- 1 ½ pounds apricots (8-10), halved and pitted
- 1 tablespoon turbinado sugar (such as Sugar In the Raw)

Special Equipment

- 10-inch cast-iron skillet

1. Preheat oven to 350°F. Coat a 10-inch cast-iron skillet with nonstick pan spray.
2. In a medium bowl, whisk together flour, baking powder, ½ teaspoon cardamom, and salt.
3. In a large bowl, use an electric mixer to beat butter and granulated sugar on medium-high speed until light and fluffy (about 5 minutes).
4. Reduce mixer speed to medium-low. Add eggs one at a time, beating well after each addition and scraping down the bowl.
5. Add almond extract and beat briefly.
6. Reduce mixer speed to low and add flour mixture, beating until just combined.
7. Spoon batter into the prepared skillet and smooth the top.
8. Arrange apricot halves on top of the batter, skin-side up, nearly covering the surface.
9. In a small bowl, mix remaining ¼ teaspoon cardamom with turbinado sugar. Sprinkle over the cake.
10. Bake for 45 minutes, or until the cake is golden, apricots are soft, and a toothpick comes out clean.
11. Cool in the skillet on a wire rack. Serve warm or at room temperature.

CRISPY CLOUD PASTRIES

Prep time: 5 minutes | **Cook time: 50 minutes** |Serves **24**

- 1 stick (½ cup) unsalted butter, cubed
- 2 tablespoons granulated sugar (optional, for sweet version)
- ½ to 1 teaspoon kosher salt (½ teaspoon for sweet version; 1 teaspoon for savory version)
- 1¼ cups all-purpose flour
- 4 large eggs

1. In a medium saucepan, combine the butter, sugar (if using), salt, and 1 cup water. Bring to a simmer over medium heat, stirring until the butter melts completely.
2. Add the flour all at once and stir vigorously with a wooden spoon. Cook, stirring constantly, until the dough forms a smooth ball and pulls away from the sides of the pan, about 30 seconds to 1 minute. A thin film of dough should form on the bottom of the pan.
3. Remove the pan from the heat and let the dough cool for 5 minutes. Transfer the dough to a large mixing bowl.
4. Using an electric mixer with the whisk attachment, beat in the eggs one at a time on medium speed. Mix until the dough is smooth and glossy after each addition.
5. Immediately transfer the dough to a pastry bag fitted with a large plain tip. If not using right away, cover with plastic wrap and refrigerate for up to 2 days.
6. Preheat the oven to 425°F. Line two baking sheets with parchment paper.
7. Pipe the dough onto the parchment in your desired shapes, leaving 1½ inches between each pastry.
8. Bake for 15 minutes, then reduce the oven temperature to 375°F. Continue baking until the pastries are golden brown and puffed, and sound hollow when tapped, about 25 minutes more.
9. Immediately pierce the shells with a small, sharp knife to release steam (this helps them stay crispy). Transfer to a wire rack to cool completely.
10. Fill with your favorite filling or store unfilled shells in an airtight container for up to 2 days.

STRAWBERRY-SHORTCAKE PARFAIT POPS

Prep time: **5 minutes** | Cook time: **20 minutes** | Freeze time: **4 hours** | Serves **6**

- Cooking spray
- 1½ cups Special K Red Berries cereal
- ½ cup unsweetened shredded coconut
- ¾ cup vanilla frozen yogurt, slightly softened
- ¾ cup strawberry sorbet, slightly softened
- 6 wooden popsicle sticks

1. Coat the insides of six 3-ounce paper cups with cooking spray.
2. In a food processor, pulse the cereal and coconut until coarsely ground.
3. Layer the ingredients in each cup:
   - Sprinkle 1 tablespoon of cereal mixture in the bottom
   - Add 1 tablespoon frozen yogurt
   - Top with 2 tablespoons sorbet
   - Press gently with the back of a spoon
   - Add another 1 tablespoon frozen yogurt
   - Sprinkle with remaining cereal mixture
4. Insert a wooden stick into the center of each pop.
5. Freeze until completely firm, at least 4 hours.
6. Just before serving, snip the sides of the paper cups with kitchen scissors and peel off.

FRUITY FROZEN YOGURT BARK

Prep time: **20 minutes** | Freeze time: **3-4 hours** | Serves: **8**

- 2 cups Greek yogurt (plain or vanilla)
- 1 tablespoon honey or maple syrup
- Assorted fresh fruits (strawberries, blueberries, kiwi, mango, etc.)
- ¼ cup granola or crushed nuts (optional)

1. Line a rimmed baking sheet with parchment paper.
2. In a mixing bowl, stir together the Greek yogurt and honey until well combined.
3. Spread the yogurt mixture evenly on the parchment-lined baking sheet, creating a thin, uniform layer.
4. Wash and prepare your chosen fruits. Slice into thin pieces or small chunks.
5. Arrange fruit slices on top of the yogurt layer. Get creative with patterns or scatter randomly.
6. If desired, sprinkle granola or crushed nuts over the fruit for added crunch.
7. Freeze for 3-4 hours, or until completely solid.
8. Remove from freezer and break into pieces using your hands or a knife.
9. Serve immediately and enjoy this refreshing, healthy treat!

FUDGY BROWNIES WITH CHOCOLATE CHIPS

Prep time: 5 minutes | Cook time: 40 minutes | Serves 12

- 2 sticks (1 cup) unsalted butter, cubed
- 1½ cups plus 3 tablespoons bittersweet chocolate chips
- 1 cup packed dark brown sugar
- ¾ cup granulated sugar
- 1¼ cups all-purpose flour
- ½ teaspoon kosher salt
- 4 large eggs
- 2 teaspoons pure vanilla extract
- 2 tablespoons cacao nibs

1. Preheat the oven to 350°F. Line a 13x9-inch metal or glass baking pan with parchment paper, leaving a few inches of overhang on the long sides. (This will help you easily lift the brownies out of the pan after baking.)
2. Create a double boiler: Place a heatproof medium bowl over a pan of simmering water, ensuring the bottom of the bowl doesn't touch the water. Combine the butter, 1½ cups of chocolate chips, brown sugar, and granulated sugar in the bowl.
3. Stir occasionally until the butter has completely melted and the mixture is smooth. Using oven mitts, carefully remove the bowl from the pan and set aside to cool slightly.
4. In a small bowl, whisk together the flour and salt.
5. In a large bowl, use an electric mixer with the whisk attachment to beat the eggs until slightly thickened, about 1½ minutes.
6. Reduce the mixer speed and beat in the vanilla and the melted chocolate mixture.
7. Using a rubber spatula, gently fold in the dry ingredients until just combined. Be careful not to overmix.
8. Spread the batter evenly in the prepared pan. Scatter the remaining 3 tablespoons of chocolate chips and the cacao nibs over the surface.
9. Bake until the brownies are glossy on top and the center resists light pressure when pressed, about 35 minutes.
10. Let the brownies cool completely in the pan on a wire rack.
11. Using the parchment paper overhang, lift the brownies out onto a cutting board and cut into 24 pieces.

NEW YORK–STYLE CHEESECAKE

Prep time: **1 hour 35 minutes** | Cook time: **1 hour 5 minutes** | Serves **16**

For the Crust:
- 1¼ cups graham cracker crumbs (from 11 crackers)
- 4 tablespoons unsalted butter, melted
- 1 tablespoon granulated sugar

For the Filling:
- 3 packages (8 ounces each) cream cheese, softened
- ¾ cup granulated sugar
- 1 tablespoon all-purpose flour
- 1½ teaspoons vanilla extract
- 3 large eggs
- 1 large egg yolk
- ¼ cup whole milk

For Garnish:
- Fresh berries (optional)

1. Preheat oven to 375°F.
2. In a medium bowl, use a fork to mix graham cracker crumbs, melted butter, and sugar until crumbs are evenly moistened.
3. Press the crumb mixture firmly into the bottom and up the sides of a 9-inch springform pan.
4. Bake for 10 minutes.
5. Cool the crust completely in the pan on a wire rack.
6. Reduce oven temperature to 300°F.
7. In a large bowl, use an electric mixer on medium speed to beat cream cheese and sugar until smooth and fluffy.
8. Beat in flour and vanilla until well combined.
9. Reduce mixer speed to low.
10. Beat in eggs and egg yolk one at a time, beating well after each addition.
11. Beat in milk just until blended.
12. Pour batter onto the prepared crust.
13. Bake for 55 to 60 minutes, or until the center is set but still slightly jiggly and moist, and the edges are pale gold.
14. Cool the cheesecake completely in the pan on a wire rack.
15. Refrigerate overnight before serving.
16. Use a small metal spatula to loosen the cake from the sides of the pan.
17. Remove the springform ring.
18. Garnish with fresh berries, if desired.

APPENDIX 1: MEASUREMENT CONVERSION CHART

MEASUREMENT CONVERSION CHART

VOLUME EQUIVALENTS(DRY)

US STANDARD	METRIC (APPROXIMATE)
1/8 teaspoon	0.5 mL
1/4 teaspoon	1 mL
1/2 teaspoon	2 mL
3/4 teaspoon	4 mL
1 teaspoon	5 mL
1 tablespoon	15 mL
1/4 cup	59 mL
1/2 cup	118 mL
3/4 cup	177 mL
1 cup	235 mL
2 cups	475 mL
3 cups	700 mL
4 cups	1 L

WEIGHT EQUIVALENTS

US STANDARD	METRIC (APPROXIMATE)
1 ounce	28 g
2 ounces	57 g
5 ounces	142 g
10 ounces	284 g
15 ounces	425 g
16 ounces (1 pound)	455 g
1.5 pounds	680 g
2 pounds	907 g

VOLUME EQUIVALENTS(LIQUID)

US STANDARD	US STANDARD (OUNCES)	METRIC (APPROXIMATE)
2 tablespoons	1 fl.oz.	30 mL
1/4 cup	2 fl.oz.	60 mL
1/2 cup	4 fl.oz.	120 mL
1 cup	8 fl.oz.	240 mL
1 1/2 cup	12 fl.oz.	355 mL
2 cups or 1 pint	16 fl.oz.	475 mL
4 cups or 1 quart	32 fl.oz.	1 L
1 gallon	128 fl.oz.	4 L

TEMPERATURES EQUIVALENTS

FAHRENHEIT(F)	CELSIUS(C) (APPROXIMATE)
225 °F	107 °C
250 °F	120 °C
275 °F	135 °C
300 °F	150 °C
325 °F	160 °C
350 °F	180 °C
375 °F	190 °C
400 °F	205 °C
425 °F	220 °C
450 °F	235 °C
475 °F	245 °C
500 °F	260 °C

The Dirty Dozen and Clean Fifteen

The Environmental Working Group (EWG) is a nonprofit, nonpartisan organization dedicated to protecting human health and the environment Its mission is to empower people to live healthier lives in a healthier environment. This organization publishes an annual list of the twelve kinds of produce, in sequence, that have the highest amount of pesticide residue-the Dirty Dozen-as well as a list of the fifteen kinds ofproduce that have the least amount of pesticide residue-the Clean Fifteen.

THE DIRTY DOZEN	THE CLEAN FIFTEEN
• The 2016 Dirty Dozen includes the following produce. These are considered among the year's most important produce to buy organic:	• The least critical to buy organically are the Clean Fifteen list. The following are on the 2016 list:

THE DIRTY DOZEN

Strawberries	Spinach
Apples	Tomatoes
Nectarines	Bell peppers
Peaches	Cherry tomatoes
Celery	Cucumbers
Grapes	Kale/collard greens
Cherries	Hot peppers

• The Dirty Dozen list contains two additional itemskale/collard greens and hot peppers-because they tend to contain trace levels of highly hazardous pesticides.

THE CLEAN FIFTEEN

Avocados	Papayas
Corn	Kiw
Pineapples	Eggplant
Cabbage	Honeydew
Sweet peas	Grapefruit
Onions	Cantaloupe
Asparagus	Cauliflower
Mangos	

• Some of the sweet corn sold in the United States are made from genetically engineered (GE) seedstock. Buy organic varieties of these crops to avoid GE produce.

APPENDIX 3: INDEX

Hey there!

Wow, can you believe we've reached the end of this culinary journey together? I'm truly thrilled and filled with joy as I think back on all the recipes we've shared and the flavors we've discovered. This experience, blending a bit of tradition with our own unique twists, has been a journey of love for good food. And knowing you've been out there, giving these dishes a try, has made this adventure incredibly special to me.

Even though we're turning the last page of this book, I hope our conversation about all things delicious doesn't have to end. I cherish your thoughts, your experiments, and yes, even those moments when things didn't go as planned. Every piece of feedback you share is invaluable, helping to enrich this experience for us all.

I'd be so grateful if you could take a moment to share your thoughts with me, be it through a review on Amazon or any other place you feel comfortable expressing yourself online. Whether it's praise, constructive criticism, or even an idea for how we might do things differently in the future, your input is what truly makes this journey meaningful.

This book is a piece of my heart, offered to you with all the love and enthusiasm I have for cooking. But it's your engagement and your words that elevate it to something truly extraordinary.

Thank you from the bottom of my heart for being such an integral part of this culinary adventure. Your openness to trying new things and sharing your experiences has been the greatest gift.

Catch you later,

Janet D. Saucedo

Made in the USA
Coppell, TX
23 December 2024

43434124R00044